OUT OF THE CLOSET
INTO OUR HEARTS

Nancy Lamkin Olson and Rev. Kurt Olson.
(see their articles on pages 77–78 and 108–110)
Photo: Jeremiah Olson

OUT OF THE CLOSET
INTO OUR HEARTS

Celebrating Our Gay/Lesbian Family Members

Edited by
Laura Siegel and Nancy Lamkin Olson

Leyland Publications
San Francisco

First edition 2001
Front cover photo by Jennifer Charney. Front cover design by Stevee Postman.

ACKNOWLEDGMENTS
"The Fault" by Sondra Zeidenstein is reprinted with permission from *Late Afternoon Woman* by Sondra Zeidenstein, copyright © 1992 Chicory Blue Press; "My Favorite Uncle" by Kia Thomas is reprinted with permission from *Out With It: Gay and Straight Teens Write About Homosexuality* copyright © 1996 by Youth Communications/New York Center, Inc. [For more information contact Young Communications, 224 W. 29th St., 2nd fl., New York, NY 10001]. "Acceptance" by Elizabeth Vickery first appeared in *Trans Forming Families: Stories About Transgendered Loved Ones*, Mary Boenke, ed. © 1999, Walter Trook Publishing and is reprinted with permission. "Passenger" by Shirley Powers first appeared in *Bound by Diversity* © 1994 by Sebastian Press and is reprinted with permission. "For the Love of Pete" copyright © by Gene Shalit, first appeared in *The Advocate*, Oct. 28, 1997.

The following material is reprinted from original publication as listed with permission of the author, or author and parents: "Tales from a Multifunctional Family" by Alison Wearing first appeared in *The Toronto Globe and Mail*, July 20, 1994; "In Our Garden" by Abby Lawton first appeared in *Just For Us*, newsletter of Colage (Children of Lesbians and Gays Everywhere); "Dear Granny" by Emily Bell first appeared in the *PFLAG Stanislaus Newsletter*; "The Bond Between Brothers" by Peter Gambaccini first appeared in *Men's Fitness* (now *Muscle and Fitness*), Aug. 1995; "A Very Special X-Chromosome" by Laura Siegel first appeared in the *San Francisco Examiner*, July 28, 1993; "I Met You at the Parade" by Bonnie Sublett first appeared in the Peninsula, CA PFLAG newsletter, May 1992; "Amazon Mama" by Jyl Safier first appeared in *Just for Us*, newsletter of Colage, Winter 1996/7; "The Pride of a Lion" by James M. Pines first appeared in *The Washington Blade*, Dec. 2, 1994 under the title, "Father Be a Lion"; "What a Waste" by Karen Torgerson Jackson first appeared in *The Greater Chicago PFLAG Newsletter*, Dec. 97–Jan. 98. "My Son Matt" by Dennis Shepard first appeared in *The Advocate*, April 3, 2000; quote by Emma Thompson first appeared in *The Advocate*, Sept. 19, 1995. Permission to reprint by Liberation Publications, Inc.

Library of Congress Cataloging-in-Publication Data

Out of the closet, into our hearts : celebrating our gay/lesbian family members / edited by Laura Siegel and Nancy Lamkin Olson.
    p. cm.
ISBN 0-943595-84-3 (alk. paper)
    1. Gay men—United States—Family relationships.   2. Lesbians—United States—Family relationships.   3. Parents of gays—United States.   4. Children of gays—United States.   I. Siegel, Laura.   II. Olson, Nancy Lamkin.

HQ76.3.U5 O96 2001
306.874—dc21   00-48410

Leyland Publications
P.O. Box 410690
San Francisco, CA 94141

CONTENTS

12 Introduction

14 Acknowledgments

I. WE'RE HERE, WE'RE FAMILY, GET USED TO US

17 Honoring My Son Morty
Jeanne Manford

20 For the Love of Pete
Gene Shalit

22 Tales from a Multifunctional Family
Alison Wearing

24 In Our Garden
Abby Lawton

25 Dear Granny
Emily Bell

26 My Favorite Uncle
Kia Thomas

30 In Awe of Brittany
Sherry Pangborn

II. WHAT'S GAY ANYWAY?

35 Mom, What's Gay?
Deb Bridge

39 A Very Special X-Chromosome
Laura Siegel

41 Just Like Everyone Else
Laura Siegel

42 Uncle Ben and Uncle Greg
Celina de Sa, Rasa de Sa, and Antar de Sa

45 I Met You at the Parade
Bonnie Sublett

47   Amazon Mama
     Jyl Safier

49   Back to the Bear World
     Melissa Pinol

56   Acceptance
     Elizabeth Vickery

58   Uncomfortable
     Duncan Zenobia Saffir

     III. EXPANDING OUR WORLD

61   Ms Razz-ma-tazz
     Rhea Murray

64   The Pride of a Lion
     James M. Pines

66   High Tea
     Virginia Chase Sutton

68   The World Needs All Kinds of Music
     Dean L. Rosen

71   What Is the Answer? What Is the Question?
     Kim Roberts

73   The Way Our Lives Are Interwoven
     Jennifer Harris

77   The Perks
     Nancy Lamkin Olson

79   Passenger
     Shirley Powers

81   Ten Reasons to Be Happy That Your Daughter Is Bisexual
     Patricia B. Campbell

82   Dia de los Muertes: A Chance to Celebrate a Loved
     One's Life
     Liz Armstrong

84   The Kvelling Grandma
     Margy Kleinerman

88 The Fault
Sondra Zeidenstein

IV. TAKING OUR FAITH SERIOUSLY

91 A Family's Blessings
Tom Starnes

93 The Heart of a Flower
Carole and Richard L. Fowler

96 Sedar Night in the Melting Pot
Dvora Luz

98 The Wedding
Norman Diamond

99 The Weaving
Linda Diamond

101 Witness
Betty Dorr

104 Spreading Light
Irma Fischer

106 Coming Out at Home
Ellen and Harold Kameya

108 Alleluia
Reverend Kurt Olson

V. . . . AND ALL WE DID WAS LOVE

113 Loving Every Minute
Joe "Papa Joe" Basile

115 Mother's Day
"Laura Lamb"

116 Not a Boo in the Bunch
Reverend Bob Hawthorne

117 Telling Mom-Mom
Jean Lin

121   The Bond Between Brothers
      Peter Gambaccini

124   A Parent Genie
      Donald J. Moran

126   What a Waste
      Karen Torgerson Jackson

128   Designer Genes
      Sondra Audin Armer

VI. I KNOW THAT YOU LOVE ME BUT WHEN I
     WALK OUT THE DOOR WHO ELSE WILL?

131   Testimony of a Really Lucky Kid
      Sol Kelley-Jones

133   A Grandfather's First Pride Parade
      Margaret DaRos

137   My Daughter—the Teenager
      Becky Sarah

138   Hineni
      Lauren Hauptman

140   Something Joyous Within Me Broke Through
      Betty Cornin

145   My Son Matt
      Dennis Shepard

  10   With quotes by *Emma Thompson*, *James Spahr and James Spahr II*, and *Betty DeGeneres*—reprinted with permission.

152   Contributors

159   The Editors

ILLUSTRATIONS

2   Nancy Lamkin Olson and Rev. Kurt Olson
16   Morty Manford and his mother Jeanne
29   Kia Thomas
34   Rick, Deb and Michael as Ophelia Coxwell
38   Stuart Siegel
48   Melissa Pinol and her brother, Grant
60   Rhea Murray and Bruce Murray
72   Pat Mayne and Jennifer Harris
80   Patricia B. Campbell and Kathryn Campbell Kibler
90   Wave Starnes, Tom Starnes, Celina Gomez, Keott Gomez-Starnes, Floyd Starnes, Carlos Gomez, Dylan Gomez-Starnes
100   Betty Dorr and son Michael
108   Christian Olson and his partner, Tom Feddor
112   Joseph Basile and his brother Steve
120   Peter Gambaccini and Paul Gambaccini
130   Joann Kelley, Sol Kelley-Jones, Sunshine Jones
144   Matthew Shepard
158   Laura Siegel; Nancy Lamkin Olson

Cover: Mike Neubecker and son Lee (see also p. 155)
Photo: Jennifer Charney

"I'm the proud father of a gay son and hope this license plate will make people think and help remove the stigma of being gay. It might be a source of hope for gay youth who have a higher risk of suicide. Gay youth have trouble accepting themselves, especially when they hear negative messages at school, home and even in their house of worship. I think the plate also shows that gay people are valued members of families who love them."

—Mike Neubecker, Brownstown Twp., Michigan

"Yes, she's a lesbian, but she's my mom and she
could love men or women as long as she was my mom
and told me what was going on.
Her honesty helps me to deal with the world."
—James Spahr II, son of Reverend Dr. Jane Adams Spahr

"I was sitting with my sons in my small apartment
in San Rafael, California and I was telling them
that their mom's picture would be in the paper the next day
and they would call her a lesbian and maybe some other words.
Chet who was nine said, 'Hey dad, somebody's gotta
be the first to ride on the front of the bus and drink from
the "Whites Only" fountain.'"
—James Spahr, former husband of Reverend Jane Adams Spahr

"My name is Betty DeGeneres and my kid is the greatest.
You know her. She's Ellen—and she's gay.
For too long, gay Americans have suffered discrimination.
As long as our sons and daughters are excluded from the basic
protection of law, we must share that burden as a family.
So let's not waste one child—and let them all reach for the stars."
—Human Rights Campaign Public Service Announcement

"My uncle was gay and so were my godfathers. I was
brought up in a very gay environment. When I was young,
the fact of their homosexuality was not hidden. It was so
much a part of my life that when I went out, as it were,
into the world and discovered that homosexuality was not
generally acceptable, I was deeply shocked. My uncle and
my godfathers absolutely had a lot to do with my upbringing
and my attitude towards life. I was really lucky."
—Emma Thompson, actress (The Advocate, 1995)

DEDICATION

To our beloved sons,
both gay and straight.
Christian and Tom, Stuart,
Jeremiah, Kevin, and Alan

Introduction

We began collecting celebratory stories by family members of gay, lesbian, bisexual, and transgendered people, to give greater voice to a population not often heard over the shouts of anger, hatred, and bigotry. How often do we hear about a mother's tender love for a daughter who has just announced, "I like girls"? ("Mother's Day" by Laura Lamb). Or about a grandfather who defends his grandson against the jeers of peer Army veterans ("A Grandfather's First Pride Parade" by Margaret DaRos). The voice of love is inherent in every one of these pieces.

We are both mothers of gay sons. Our children have enriched our lives beyond measure. They have introduced us to a vibrant, loving, and passionate community. Our children (collectively speaking) have taken us to our first drag performance as Rhea Murray delightfully describes in "Ms Razz-ma-tazz." They have introduced us to Gay Pride Celebrations and shown us how to receive more love than we ever knew possible ("I Met You at the Parade" by Bonnie Sublett). They have even let us ride on the back of motorcycles with Dykes on Bikes ("Passenger" by Shirley Powers).

These writers also show us a quieter kind of love. In fact, most of these pieces describe a love that we don't often see on the front page of newspapers. The love of a family sharing Christmas dinner together is described by Tom Starnes in "A Family's Blessings." The love and respect of two cousins who buy matching cloaks becomes a visible symbol of "The Way Our Lives Are Interwoven" (Jennifer Harris). And there's the love of a mother, Karen Torgerson Jackson ("What a Waste"), who manages to spend an entire day with her daughter without saying the word "lesbian" once. These are ordinary stories of love and celebration that are also extraordinary in a world that constantly attempts to disenfranchise our family members.

We have also written this book as a gift to all gay, lesbian, bisexual and transgendered people—to tell them they are indeed loved and celebrated. They are celebrated fiercely ("The Pride of a Lion" by James Pines). They are celebrated compassionately ("The Heart of a Flower" by Carole and Richard L. Fowler) and they are celebrated in the presence of God ("Alleluia" by Reverend Kurt A. Olson).

They are celebrated on the floor of the legislature ("Testimony" by 10-year-old Sol Kelley-Jones), at church ("Witness" by Betty Dorr) and at school ("Something Joyous Within Me Broke Through" by Betty Cornin).

We family members are literally bursting out of our closets. As the religious right shouts, "Gays are leading sinful lives," as full page newspaper ads state, "Gays can be cured"; these writers proclaim, "We are thrilled that our family members are gay, lesbian, bisexual and transgendered. We wouldn't want them to 'be' any other way."

Many people have the perception that having a gay, lesbian, bisexual or transgendered family member is a problem to be overcome. Many people indeed go through various stages of denial, grief, anger, and fear. We have also collected these stories for families who are struggling—to show them what is possible if they open their hearts and simply love.

These stories show that it is not only possible to celebrate our gay, lesbian, bisexual and transgendered family members—it is natural, basic, and inherent in the family relationship.

Some of the contributors to this anthology refer to an organization called PFLAG (Parents, Families and Friends of Lesbians and Gays). PFLAG promotes the health and well-being of gay, lesbian, bisexual and transgendered persons, their families and friends through: support, to cope with an adverse society; education, to enlighten an ill-informed public; and advocacy, to end discrimination and to secure civil rights. PFLAG provides an opportunity for dialogue about our sexual orientation and gender identity, and acts to create a society that is healthy and respectful of human diversity. Serving over 80,000 members, PFLAG affiliates are located in more than 445 communities across the United States, and abroad. Whether you are gay, lesbian, bisexual, transgendered or a family member, PFLAG needs your support and presence to further its mission.

This anthology represents the voices of over 50 mothers, fathers, grandparents, siblings, children, nieces, nephews, and cousins; however, there are many more family members out there who celebrate. We encourage you to continue doing the most important job you can possibly do in your life—to show another person that they are loved, supported, and valued. And if the feeling strikes you to one day express that love publicly—*do it!!* Join PFLAG, write letters, march in pride parades, speak out. That love and outreach will return to you in ways you never imagined. That love can reduce the risk of AIDS, suicide and drug use. If gay, lesbian, bisexual and transgendered people are valued and celebrated, they will have a reason to love and celebrate themselves.

One of the contributors to this anthology, Laura Lamb, has used a pseudonym out of respect for her daughter who is not yet "out" at high school. Another contributor, Dennis Shepard, honors his son Matthew after Matthew's brutal murder. We, the editors, hope that one day all gay, lesbian, bisexual and transgendered people will be able to live with more openness and acceptance—that they no longer need to live in fear of coming out or being harmed. We see the day when stories like these will be the standard by which young gay, lesbian, bisexual and transgendered people can be accepted and loved.

—Laura Siegel & Nancy Lamkin Olson

Acknowledgments

We would like to thank Race Bannon and Richard Labonte for the help they gave us in the early stage of this anthology's conception.

Thank you to Lani Ka'ahumanu, Cheri Long, and Shannon Nottestad for being the best cheerleaders ever—for having faith in the project from the very beginning and for encouraging us to stick with it.

Thank you to Felicia Park-Rogers for helping us gather stories written by the children of gay and lesbian parents.

We would also like to thank our husbands, Howard Siegel and Kurt Olson for their love and encouragement. Their belief in our book and its message is a continuous source of support and strength.

Thank you to our publisher Winston Leyland for his patience and belief in our message.

And special gratitude to the spirit of James Bergeron III who believed that writing our stories is the most important and powerful thing one can do.

I

WE'RE HERE, WE'RE FAMILY,
GET USED TO US

new york **MATTACHINE**

35¢

JULY/AUG 1972

Times

Morty Manford (left) and his mother Jeanne (carrying sign) marching
in New York City's Christopher Street Liberation Day Parade, June
1972. Photo: Manuscripts and Archives Division, New York Public
Library. Mort Manford Papers. Astor, Lenox and Tilden Foundations

Honoring My Son Morty

Jeanne Manford

My son Morty was present at the Stonewall bar in New York City's Greenwich Village on the night it was raided and riots erupted. Anger reached a peak over unfair harassment and prejudice of gay people. They had had enough and rebelled; the riots continued into the next day.

Stonewall was the birth of the fight for gay civil rights. It was the start of the revolution for fair treatment of gay people. They were going to fight discrimination in jobs, housing and all areas.

Although my family and I were unaware of Stonewall at that time, those few days in June 1969 were to open new horizons for us and enrich and change our lives.

Morty joined the Gay Activist Alliance whose focus was the enactment of civil rights legislation in the New York City Council. Shortly after that, the *New York Daily News* had an article entitled "Any Old Jobs for Homos?" that went on and on about "fairies, nancys, tweekers, fags, lezzies, etc." It was outrageous.

I knew my gay son was not only normal, but a superior person in every aspect. I was outraged that people didn't think that he should be given equal treatment.

One night I got a phone call saying that my son had been arrested. The police officer, expecting to shock me, said, "You know, your son is homosexual."

I replied, "Yes, I know. Why are you bothering him? Why don't you go after criminals and stop harassing gays?"

At that time, the Inner Circle, an annual get together of the press and politicians was held at the Hilton Hotel. Morty and his friends distributed leaflets protesting media oppression. A number of gay men ended up in the hospital, Morty among them. He was beaten up by Michael May, president of the firemen's union and a Golden Gloves boxing champion. Although May was identified by important city officials at a trial, he was not convicted.

I was furious! The police stood by and did nothing. I wrote a letter to *The New York Post* and it was printed. Morty called me the next morning and said his friends were calling him up. I was the talk of the gay community. No parent had ever stated publicly that she had a gay child.

I wrote to the paper because I loved my son and never thought of hiding the fact that he was gay. I am a shy person, but I was not going to let people walk all over Morty.

After that, my husband and I were asked to speak on radio and TV, and at rallies. We realized that speaking out could help other parents understand that they were the bridge between the gay and heterosexual communities and that we could help our children receive what the Constitution guaranteed.

In June 1972, Morty asked me to march in the Christopher Street Liberation Day Parade (as it was called then) in New York City. I said that I would march if I could carry a sign. What good is it for a person to march if people don't know why you are marching?

I carried a sign, "Parents of Gays Unite in Support for Our Children." The crowds screamed as we walked by. I thought they were screaming at Dr. Benjamin Spock, who was walking behind us. But they were cheering me. They kissed me and asked me to speak to their parents. As we walked, Morty and I discussed the idea of starting a group for parents.

On March 11, 1973, we had our first meeting. There were about 20 people present. The thrust of those meetings was for parents and society to understand that there was nothing to be ashamed of if their child was homosexual. Diversity is wonderful. Gays are not inferior to heterosexuals. In fact, very often the opposite is true.

I remember thinking that day that someday we could expand and help our children politically and educate the world, but first we had to help families. Several decades later that dream has been realized, and we still have much work to do.

My husband and son are gone now. There are, however, many wonderful memories. For instance, the day after my husband Jules marched in his first June gay pride parade in 1973, a nurse that he knew came up to him and said, "Thank you, Dr. Manford." A former student whom I taught in fifth grade called to tell me that when he realized he was gay, he felt it was all right because Mrs. Manford's son was gay too.

My son Morty was a hero; he was compassionate and fearless. I feel Morty's presence with me as I say that it is up to all of us to carry on with renewed vigor the work done by Morty and all of the early gay activists.

For the Love of Pete

Gene Shalit

My eldest son, Peter, is a physician, he's gay, he and his partner have been together for 17 years, and I wish we'd see
each other more often. (You call 3,000 miles far?) He graduated
from the University of Washington Medical School in Seattle,
where he now lectures and has a private practice; he is a Ph.D. in
genetics; he was Phi Beta Kappa at Cornell as an undergraduate;
he was a prodigy in botany, beginning to grow plants at age 6; he
wrote for botanical journals at 12; and he is currently finishing
a book about gay men's health. Among other areas of expertise,
he is an authority on AIDS, with a great many patients, and was
among a small team of physicians who went before the Washington State Supreme Court on the side of allowing doctor-assisted
death. Peter is humane and intelligent, and I'm crazy about him.
(One of the nice things about me is that I never brag about my
kids.)

One day, home from Cornell, he asked me to his room, where
he announced that he is gay. I replied along the lines of, "I thought
you had something important to tell me." However, he says I was
far from indifferent. Since this was some two decades ago, perhaps
each of us has his own mirror of memory. Peter says I was extremely concerned about his physical safety and the consequences
to his career. He may very well be right, but I would have had
good cause. Remember, it was 1973, not 1997. (And 1997 ain't
so hot either.) Open bigotry was far more widespread. Many of
today's empty closets were then crowded. It would have been unnatural for me not to have been concerned. I was also frightened
when my younger photographer son went to El Salvador and
Nicaragua during the worst of the civil wars. Do I love them both?
You bet.

Peter has asked if I wondered if his upbringing resulted in his
being gay. I can't imagine it (although he says we definitely discussed it), any more than my daughter's upbringing resulted in her

being left-handed or a third son's turning into a computer whiz who's a vegetarian and writer and digs gurus from India. My six children are individuals working in diverse fields. In Peter's case I rarely think about his being gay unless it's brought up, any more than I ponder my other children's being evidently heterosexual. Some of my best friends are heterosexuals. If I have any regret, it is that Peter has no children. He would have terrific kids, and he'd be a wonderful father.

I have covered the performing arts for network TV and national magazines for almost 50 years. Women and men in theater, film, music, art, and dance exhibit every kind of personal proclivity. As a critic, I don't judge individuals; I judge an individual's work. Groups are mosaics: there are wonderful Norwegians and awful Norwegians, good Episcopalians and boring Episcopalians, nice gays and gross gays, lousy presidents and great presidents.

Many parents lie awake at night wondering if they played a role in the sexual orientation of their children. I think they should go back to sleep. Each child is an individual. Speaking personally, mine are in constant touch with their brothers and sisters, and their love for each other is the most joyous aspect in my life.

My credo has always been: Let children follow their own star.

Tales from a Multifunctional Family

Alison Wearing

My father and stepmother have been together for 13 years. They met, ahem, in a bar. My father spotted my stepmother, plopped himself on the next bar stool and opened with the line, "So . . . what have you been up to tonight?" Miraculously, a conversation ensued. They spent the rest of the evening talking about opera.

The next morning, my stepmother handed my father a telephone number and said, "Now *call me*."

A year later, they moved in together. Now they have two dogs and a subscription to *Opera* magazine. But they're not your average couple. They're both fulfilled. In fact, they have the sort of relationship I admire. They are two distinct individuals who are in each other's company simply because they adore it.

They're also not your average couple because they're both men. Which means that my stepmother is actually more of a fairy stepmother, if you know what I mean.

My father "came out" in the late seventies. It was more than anyone was ready for. Most of his immediate family disowned him—apparently they'd rather see him a miserable hetero than a jubilant homo—and everyone else took a giant step back. There were a lot of hushed tones around the neighborhood. Pitying stares from the neighbors. The telephone went silent. Dinner parties stopped. I felt like our house had been quarantined.

I was 13 when I was told, "Your father loves men." Having grown up in a small town in Southern Ontario, I was unprepared for this news. I thought it meant that my father loved my brothers and not me. But that didn't last long. You'd be surprised how quickly kids can figure things out.

I hated being told that I came from a dysfunctional family (and, it was implied, that I should therefore prepare for a life of crime and general misery), by people whose "functional" families seemed often to be cesspools of muzzled emotions. And I never understood why it was okay that some fathers were sexist, beer-guzzling sport thugs but the fact that mine was a mild-mannered opera queen was unacceptable. I decided to refuse everyone else's definition of normal. I liked mine better.

Today, I look around and breathe a sigh of relief, grateful to have been exposed to alternative lifestyles at such a young age. Imagine being given the opportunity to question traditional relationships before you are old enough to get into one.

I hold my father and Michael's relationship in very high regard. In many ways, I emulate it, though as an incurable heterosexual. They never fall into traditional roles, because there aren't any.

Having a gay father means that I am surrounded by charming, attractive men. None of whom is trying to pick me up. Having a gay father also means that I can talk to him about my sex life. And he understands. Occasionally, he offers advice; and get this—it's helpful.

Okay, okay. He's a father like any other. He never runs out of financial advice, he worries when I travel, and he is anxious for me to settle down and find a "real" job.

Lately he's even starting asking about grandchildren.

In Our Garden

Abby Lawton

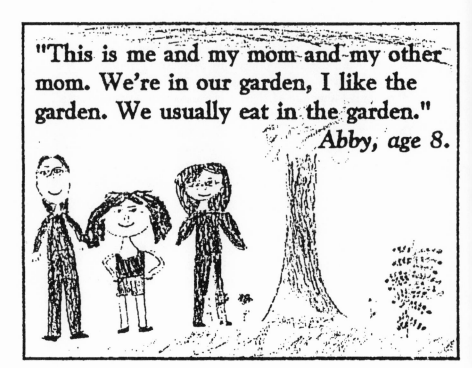

"This is me and my mom and my other mom. We're in our garden, I like the garden. We usually eat in the garden."

Abby, age 8.

Dear Granny

Emily Bell

☆ Dear Granny

heard you are getting Married
this News has really stered up
our school. you are the talk of
the town. everyone wants to Ø K,
w. "IS MY Grandma really gay"?
Of coursshe is wat is wrong
with that.

                    Love♡-EMILY

My Favorite Uncle

Kia Thomas

I always knew there was something quite different about my uncle. When I was little I even wondered how he could be an uncle at all when to my eyes, he acted and looked just like a woman. My uncle would spend a long time at the mirror doing his hair, plucking his eyebrows, putting different facial creams on his face and shaping his lips with lip liner—things I considered feminine. I even remember asking him why he never wore a skirt like other women.

It wasn't until I was around 6 that I realized that my uncle really was a man. A couple of years later I figured out that one of the things that was different about him was that he liked other men. I would wonder why he and his male friends acted like a man and a woman do—not sexually but just in terms of the closeness that they had with each other.

The fact that my uncle is gay never upset me because in my family it was always accepted. If anything, my uncle's being gay has helped me. Every time I am having guy problems, he's the one I go to for advice because I know he'll understand.

I think I cherish our relationship so much because, out of all my family, my uncle is the only one who understands what it is like to be a teenager. In some ways he is still like a teenager himself. My uncle has a different attitude on life than most adults. Unlike my "boring" parents, he has never settled down. He hangs out with his friends just like I do. He still goes out to clubs and parties till all times of the night. I've heard the saying, "gay people have more fun" and, at least in my uncle's case, that's true.

He also has a crazy sense of humor. If you do something stupid like I tend to do, he makes sure everybody in the family hears about it over and over again. My father is his favorite target. He's the oldest brother and my uncle loves to talk about how old he acts. He is always telling me, "Your father is jealous of me because he's old and bitter and I am young and lovely." In spite of the jokes, their relationship is very close.

My uncle doesn't just keep me entertained. He also listens to my problems and gives me advice when I need it. For instance, this past summer I was seeing a guy six years older than me and my parents didn't like it. My mother stopped trusting me even though she didn't have a reason to and my father treated me like a child who was unable to have her own life. It was the worst time of my life because it seemed as though my family had turned against me.

The only person I could talk to was my uncle. I told him all about the guy things I didn't tell anybody else. I asked him if I should continue to see him or call it quits because my family disapproved of our friendship. My uncle told me to do what was best for me because nobody can live my life but Kia. He also said that if I wasn't doing anything wrong then I shouldn't let my parents upset me. I followed his advice and did what I thought was best for me.

In early 1991, I found out something that has changed my life. I was sitting on my grandmother's bed doing nothing when my mother came in the room and told me that she had something to tell me. My curious ears perked up instantly. She looked at me and said, "What I am about to tell you will upset you." I immediately panicked. She told me that my uncle had been diagnosed as having HIV, the virus that causes AIDS. "He doesn't want you to know," she told me. "So don't say anything until he tells you."

I felt as though my whole world had collapsed. I was really upset and started crying but I agreed to keep quiet. What I did do was try and make it easier for him to tell me. Every time I was around him I would casually mention the topic of AIDS.

One day, about a month after my mother confided in me, my uncle and I were driving in the car and I casually mentioned that I was taking a class that discussed AIDS. I waited a few minutes to see what his reaction would be. He didn't say anything. Then I told him a few of the facts that I had learned. Again I waited. This time he said, "Did your mother tell you I have AIDS?"

I pretended that I hadn't known. But hearing it from him made it seem much more real. I was shocked but I didn't let him know. I decided to drop the subject because all of a sudden I felt uncomfortable talking about it. I had a feeling that from that day on my uncle and I would become even more close. And I was right, we have.

Last year my uncle decided to move to St. Croix for relaxation and peace. When he left it felt as though all the humor had been taken out of our family. There were no more jokes, no more gossip, nobody around to make fun of my father, no one to laugh with, and no more advice. There was also no one to help me release the stress I got from my overprotective parents.

When it finally became too much for me to bear, I got on a plane to St. Croix. When I got there, I had the time of my life. We rented a jeep and every day we went to the beach. My uncle introduced me to a friend of his who is a lesbian. What a pair they made! I remember sitting on the bed watching videos while the two of them sat there and filled me in on who was a "queen" or a "dyke." In all the years I have been in school, I have never received an education quite like the one I got on that trip.

Luckily for me, my uncle returned from St. Croix a few months ago because the family thought it would be better to have him close to home in case he got sick. He decided to go down to St. Croix every three months instead of living there year-round.

Finding out about my uncle's illness hasn't really changed our relationship. He is still the same person. The only thing that has changed is that I value the time we spend together more. Everything we do I treasure because I have learned that in life there are no guarantees. However, I still treat him the same as I always did. Maybe because I can't or don't want to fully accept what happened.

The rest of my family has reacted a little bit differently than I have. They've become more possessive and protective of him. These days, my poor uncle is being treated the same way my parents treat me.

My father is the worst. I understand that he is concerned about his younger brother but he tends to go overboard. One day we were in the car going to the bakery and every two minutes he would look at my uncle in the rear view mirror and ask if he was okay. I know this was getting on my uncle's nerves but he acted like it wasn't.

When the two of us go out now, the whole family tells me,

"Don't keep your uncle out too long because he will get tired." I want to tell them that he is a grown man with a mind of his own, but I keep it to myself because it is none of my business. My uncle doesn't say anything. I guess he doesn't want to hurt their feelings by telling them to get a life.

Since I found out about my uncle's diagnosis, I have become more aware of HIV and AIDS. People are dying every day, every minute. My uncle told me the best way to ensure my safety is to practice abstinence or safer sex. He told me there is not a man in the world worth dying for. I agree 100 percent.

Sometimes I get sad if I think about my uncle not being here. I do two things when this happens—I pray to God to protect him and then I picture him talking about somebody (usually my father) and that makes me start to laugh to myself. That makes me start to feel like he's not going anywhere.

I even told my uncle that I know he will be sitting in the first row when I graduate from high school and from college. I also informed him that he has no choice but to come to my wedding. And, knowing me and how long that will take, I can guarantee my uncle will live for a very long time.

KIA THOMAS

In Awe of Brittany

Sherry Pangborn

Brittany was my first "blood" relative, the only person in my world who was actually connected to me through birth, for I was an adopted child. From the moment I first held her in the hospital, I was possessed and madly in love with her. That feeling has continued for twenty years. Britt also is my only biological child, although I have two other beautiful daughters and one son, all adopted. I love them no less than Britt. One loves each child for his or her uniqueness, and each child brings a different sweetness and fullness to the life of a parent.

Britt was 16 and I was almost 50 when she came to us and told us that she was gay. The years since that moment have been a time of growth and change for me and my husband, a time during which we have laughed and cried and reached out more than any other time in our lives. We've done so with a sense of wonder and gratitude, feeling that our daughter opened many doors for us. In a way, it's much what Alice experienced when she fell down the rabbit hole! I think the earth opened up under us emotionally, and we were catapulted through a long tunnel to another plane of existence! Britanny took us by the hand and led us through the first months, patiently explaining and introducing us to her world. She introduced us to gay and lesbian friends, both adults and teens, and told us about their coming out processes, if indeed they had come out. She made us aware of how "invisible" some of these friends had to be in order to stay in their homes or their jobs. We read *Out* and *The Advocate* and a magazine that is now called *Curve*, all periodicals that tell what is happening in the gay communities all over the country and world.

There was never any thought of rejection in our minds. We *wanted* to understand what being gay meant to her life and to her future. Who would hire her? What kinds of positions would be receptive to an openly lesbian woman? Would she "settle down" with one person, or would her life now have to be a series of relationships, none of them permanent? Would this daughter who adores children never have any of her own? Slowly the answers came to us as we got to know the gay community in our area. Brittany could be whatever she wanted for herself in the future. She could be as "out" or as "invisible" as she felt inclined to be. She could fall in love and commit her life to another woman, have children or not. It was very much as it had been when we had perceived her as "straight." It was up to her to make her choices and to live with them as best she could. The caliber of her life would still depend on the content of her character, and on her own personal choices. She could be happy and fulfilled and accomplish whatever was within her reach, whether she was gay or straight. The obstacles and stumbling blocks would be put there either by an intolerant society, or by her own perceptions which might limit her. Either way, it seemed to us that Brittany could count on our love and support and we could still envision a happy and meaningful life for her.

We have struggled ever since with the knowledge that there are families who turn to stone in fear of their gay children, and reject them the moment they find out their sexual orientation isn't what the parents assumed it was. How can they forget the hours, days, and years that they cherished with their babies, toddlers, children, teens and young adults? The countless times they held their hands and protected them when they were afraid, the little kisses and hugs given freely.

I only know that I was always in awe of Brittany, and I still am, perhaps even more so now that I know she is gay, and realize that she lived with that knowledge for four or five years before telling us her secret. She's not only all the things that I always wanted her to be, good, kind, bright, interested in life and in others, but she's also incredibly brave and giving and forgiving!

What child should grow up and have to feel afraid to tell her parents that she's gay? What adolescent should have to shepherd her parents through life's little detours when she should be experiencing her own discoveries and joys? What teenager should have to put her arm around her parents and assure them that "everything will be okay" when it's the *parent* who should be offering reassurances?

Brittany did all this and more. I celebrate her because she's awesome and because she's beautiful and brave and so incredibly loving! I celebrate her because she can't walk by a homeless person on the sidewalk without saying hello.

I celebrate her because she has given so much joy and happiness to her family and friends, and because she makes her Dad and I glow when we think of her. I like the way she conducts her life, with confidence and dignity and pride in who she is. When I see her and her Dad march by in the Pride Parade in Seattle, I feel my heart swell up and my eyes get teary, and I'm so glad to be a part of her life!

She's my daughter! I'll always be proud of her, and I'll always love her with the same intensity. She has never made us ashamed of her in any way; she has always been the kind of person I would like to be. She's full of joy, and sorrow. She knows the difference. She understands the balance of give and take, and she's given me a lifetime of memories to cherish! I celebrate everything about her. And besides, she sings like Joan Baez and laughs like a hyena!

II

WHAT'S GAY ANYWAY?

Left to right: Rick, Deb and Michael as Ophelia Coxwell.
Photo: Keith Nicholas Diamond, Calgary

Mom, What's Gay?

Deb Bridge

Well, the word's out—I'm the 45-year-old straight mom of a 20-year-old gay son, my only child, and I'm *proud* of him. I've always been proud of Michael, and for many reasons. He's a talented writer, musician, dancer, artist, fashion designer and, most recently, maker of beautiful woven/braided leather floggers. He's intelligent, kind, sensitive, and articulate. He doesn't smoke, do drugs, or drink to excess.

But what makes me most proud of Michael is his courage and pride in himself as a gay man. He is my hero, and he's inspired me, his straight old excitable mom, to become an outspoken gay rights advocate.

What does it mean to be the proud parent of a gay child?

It means being brave and selfless enough to send him off, at the tender age of 15, to the National Ballet School (in the heart of Toronto's gay community) to pursue his dream.

It means hearing about all the ups and downs of the latest boyfriend and trying to provide comfort, advice, and emotional support to someone who's 3400 miles away and only calls home twice a week (if we're lucky).

It means having a phone bill that rivals Canada's national debt.

It means bragging to anyone who'll listen about his latest accomplishment, whether it's gay-related or not.

Sometimes it means saying (usually when I show the picture of his bare butt in the 1996 Toronto Pride Parade to an unsuspecting colleague), "Oh I'm sorry! Didn't you know Michael is gay?"

It means going to the Calgary International Airport at Christmas, so excited about his coming home that I'm jumping up and down like an idiot before he's even off the plane. Then the gates open, and behind a small group of passengers, I spot a creature in a feather headdress, white sequin-trimmed formal, and 6-inch spike heels. It's Michael, and he's in drag! Oops—not Michael—Ophelia Coxswell, who arrived at the Toronto airport in jeans and t-shirt, then transformed himself in a Canadian Airlines 747 bathroom at 37,000 feet. What a kid! . . . but as I embrace him, I can feel him shaking like a leaf. As I said, he's got courage.

This year, it means marching by his side in the Calgary Pride Parade. Last year, his impatience and long legs and my smoker's cough and short legs prevented us from marching together for long.

It's not as though I was completely unprepared, as many parents are, for his coming out.

When he was almost 5 and I was a divorced single parent finishing my B.A. in Lethbridge, one of Michael's favorite TV shows was "Three's Company" (the late-70s/early 80s sitcom with Jack and Janet and Chrissy. Jack is straight, but the landlord's been told that he's gay so the trio can be roommates.)

One Friday after we'd bussed home, Michael and I sat down to watch the show. It was an episode whose plot revolved around Jack's supposedly being gay.

When it ended, Michael looked at me and said, "Mom, what's gay?"

I said, "Well, honey, gay is when you love another man."

He chirped, "Oh! Then I guess I'm gay!"

I asked, "Why do you say that, hon?"

Michael: "Because I love dad." (my ex-husband)

Me: "That's great, dear, but being gay isn't quite like that. Being gay is loving another man and wanting to be with him like a man and a woman do when they live together or get married."

Michael, after a brief pause to mull this over: "Oh . . . then I guess I'm not gay. What's for supper?"

That evening, after Michael was in bed, I called my best friend in Red Deer and told her about this conversation. She said, "Well? What would you do?"

Ever slow on the pickup, I queried, "What do you mean, what would I do? About what?"

"What would you do if he is gay?"

"I'd love him, of course. I'd just love him."

And so I have. Through the many stages of his growing into adulthood, including the dark, dark time after he told his best

A Very Special X-Chromosome

Laura Siegel

Scientists at the National Institutes of Health have discovered that a portion of the mother's X-chromosome carries genetic material linked to homosexuality in men.

I always knew I had something to do with my child being gay.

For about 24 hours after my son told me he was gay, I thought it was because I breast-fed him too long. Perhaps he was gay because I held him too long.

Then I spoke to a few friends and professionals who convinced me I had nothing to do with his sexual orientation.

I didn't quite believe them. Not that I didn't believe in the birth theory ("My child was born that way; he didn't choose to be gay"). I just didn't want to let go of my personal involvement. I knew that in some way I was responsible. Never, however, did I express this politically incorrect belief.

Some parents fret because they believe it was their "fault."

"Fault" was not in my reasoning. My conviction had more to do with my belly. As a mother, I often "know" what is true between me and my child.

It's not easy to put into words. It's more of a flutter. Perhaps it's the same flutter I felt when he turned in his amniotic sac. Or the same flutter I feel today when I realize how much I love him.

We women are taught to be removed from our natural instincts. I was not encouraged to breast feed (I did anyway) or to give birth naturally (I didn't—I had anesthesia). But I did know how happy and peaceful I felt when I lay still and felt my son moving inside me. And I did "know" inside, years later, that he was gay because of me.

I might as well say it now. I think that gay people are special. To a friend who also has a gay son, I say, "Gay people are more creative, spirited and have a zest for life."

She disagrees and says that gay people are just like everyone else. They work, pay taxes and rear children.

I agree. But these qualities come from the father's genetic material. I'm convinced that my son's leather jacket with all the political stickers, his earrings and his backwards red baseball cap came from me, that X-chromosome only a mother can supply.

The NIH study also says that historically there are more homosexual people on the mother's side of the family than the father's. This troubled me for less than 24 hours.

I couldn't think of anyone gay on my side of the family.

Yet how do I really know? How do I know that my great-grandmother in Russia didn't cuddle with another woman, subversively, in the snow?

The NIH study also asks the question, "Why would nature select this gene on the mother's X-chromosome when two people of the same sex can't produce offspring?"

The answer is simple for me. It's my gene. And I don't particularly care if I have grandchildren. I already raised two babies. I already went through the phase of "Aren't babies adorable?"

Perhaps nature is telling me that it's time to move on.

All in all, I'm grateful to the NIH for its scientific finding. Finally I understand the depth of my belief. I always knew it was in my genes that my son would be special. I feel honored.

Just Like Everyone Else

Laura Siegel

His lips are voluptuous & red.
He wears a short flowered rayon dress.
He has a black beauty mark on his left cheekbone;
    his Elvira hair is black silk.

His auburn hair is cut short for his new job.
He wears studied copper spectacles.
He buys six pinstripe shirts & pleated cotton slacks.

Perhaps you've seen him around town
    at the parade discos bars
    working out at Gold's Gym
He was Mr. May in the 1990 bare chested calendar.
Perhaps you've seen him riding his 10 spd bike
down Market Street eating at the Spaghetti Factory
    wrapping his leftovers
    to give to the homeless

He works at an AIDS organization
He works as a volunteer for People with AIDS
Perhaps you've seen him demonstrating
    in front of Burroughs Wellcome
    marching for lower AZT prices

He's tall & slim, muscular & tan
He eats oatmeal for breakfast
    & loves elegant French cuisine

He's unique, special, different,
common, bright, a star, a jewel,
trashy, serious, white
middle class, struggling.
He's like everyone else
    ALIVE & WILLING

HE'S MY SON!

41

Uncle Ben and Uncle Greg

Celina de Sa, Rasa de Sa, and Antar de Sa
As told to Ann Davidson, their grandmother

The following is an "interview" that I had with my three grandchildren about their two Uncles, Ben and Greg. Ben is my son and he lives with his partner, Greg.

Initially, I asked all three of my grandchildren how Ben and Greg are special people in our family.

CELINA (age 8):

Uncle Ben and Uncle Greg are very special and gifted people. They're nice and I have a lot of fun with them. They take me to movies and restaurants.

They give us a $20-a-month book allowance so we can experience different kinds of books as well as different authors and how they write. No one else in my family ever does that.

We can learn different things. Some books could be about animals and some about fairy tales from different countries. There's a lot to learn in books. Ben and Greg love books. They have hundreds of books.

Ben and Greg take us to restaurants like the Peninsula Creamery and La Azteca, my favorite Mexican restaurant.

I have a book about a restaurant called *Fanny at Chez Panisse*. That's a famous restaurant. Fanny and her mom own Chez Panisse. I've heard they have a cafe and special tables where you can eat with your hands. Ben and Greg have been there before and they want to take me sometime.

Ben and Greg are really silly. They call us funny names. They call me "Ce-LAIN-a." They speak in funny voices. One time Rasa and I were playing babies and we couldn't think of any names so Greg thought of Debbie and Donna. I was Donna and Rasa was Debbie.

When we went to Ben and Greg's house, Greg was the Dad and Ben was the Mom and we acted babyish. Then when they bought

42

us treats they said, "Only big girls like Celina and Rasa can have treats." So we changed back into Celina and Rasa and got our treats. After we ate them, we changed back into Debbie and Donna, the babies, again. We can be really silly with Ben and Greg.

We put on plays with them and write scripts. Sometimes they're in the plays and sometimes they're in the audience. I write the scripts on Ben and Greg's computers.

They always rent movies and we watch them late at night. We have our very own room and our own bed and our own little bathroom at their house. Ben and Greg sleep downstairs and in the morning we crawl down the stairs and we wake them up and tell them our dreams. Then we take our showers and get dressed and eat breakfast and start fun things.

RASA (age 3-1/2):
Ben and Greg call us backwards names. I'm "Asar."

They swing us around. Sometimes they take my hand and my leg and swing me around. Fast. Really fast. I get dizzy and fall on the ground. In the grass.

We go to La Azteca and eat burritos. Before we eat we wash our hands.

We put on shows and Ben and Greg are in the audience. My Mom is in the audience too. They clap and cheer.

When we spend the night at their house we play with toys. We saw a dog named Malcolm. Malcolm jumped on me. He lives upstairs.

ANTAR (age 11):
They're really nice. They take us places when my mom can't. Like one time my mom said she was going to take me to see *Men in Black* but my dad got sick. I was kind of mad but then Ben and Greg took me. They take us to movies all the time.

Ben and Greg made me a wonderful birthday card on my last birthday. It had all these words describing me. It was a whole page of weird words, all compliments. They picked one word and then they squished all the synonyms out of it, like "cool, cool to know, cool to see, cool to be with, great, smart."

Ben and Greg stick up for me. They tell my mom not to yell at me sometimes when my mom is unfair. Like when I want to go somewhere and my mom doesn't take me seriously. I ask them if they'll talk to my mom because they have, like you know, a stronger voice. Like to my mom.

When I'm home alone, they say I can call them any time. They say, "If you get lonely or have a problem, you can always call us."

Their upstairs neighbors are lesbians and they have a dog and three cats. Their dog is named Malcolm and he's a pit bull. They found him when he was little and they adopted him. He's really nice but kind of scary too. When you play with him he opens his mouth and starts licking and licking you.

Ben and Greg spoil us a lot. Aside from the fact that they're gay, they're pretty much the same as anybody else. They just don't find women attractive. Well, they do, but you know . . . they don't think about women in the same way. They think about guys that way.

I tell my friends, "I don't care if you say people are gay. What's the problem?" And they go, "oh, blah, blah." And I say, "My uncle is gay." And they go, "Oh, huh?" Everyone looks at me and then sometimes other kids say, "Oh, my cousin is gay or my uncle is gay too."

Once I saw a cartoon. The kid had a dog and everyone called his dog gay. People said, "Get away from me. You're a gay dog." The dog runs away because it's sad. The kid gets mad and he goes looking for the dog. He finds the dog and he doesn't care if he's gay. He tells everyone, "I don't care if my dog is gay."

It was really stereotyped but it was kind of funny because the dog came up with a pink ribbon around its neck and it was a boy dog. Although people were mean and were stereotyping you could sort of get the moral of the story.

I Met You at the Parade

Bonnie Sublett

We had arranged to meet at the Parade, somewhere on Market Street between Montgomery and Powell. It was my first Gay Pride Parade. How, I wondered, would I find you in a crowd of 250,000 people?

In the minutes before the parade began, I searched through the groups of people that ebbed and flowed around the corner where I stood with the PFLAG group. No luck. I saw other young men and women, sometimes in outlandish outfits. I saw tee-shirts with messages like Lavender Diaper Dad, Lesbian, Lesbian's Lover, Lesbian's Mother, Project Aris, on and on. But still I didn't find you.

Suddenly it was our turn to move out. The PFLAG contingent took their place to cheers and whistles from a group of young people near us. Their shouts of encouragement buoyed me, but I wondered where you were.

I was still apprehensive as we turned the corner on to Market Street. Cheers rose louder and louder as we walked on. I couldn't believe my eyes. Whole blocks of people stood and cheered wildly as our band of moms, dads, grandmas, grandpas, sisters, brothers, and friends passed.

Tentatively at first, and then with increasing abandon and joy, I began to wave at the crowds. People were blowing kisses to us and yelling "Hi, Mom," and "Can I be your kid, too?" and most touching of all, "Thank you."

Then it happened. My searching eyes found you. There you were in the smiles of two elderly gay men waving shyly. They were old enough to be my own dad, but for that minute I felt like their mom, proud of their integrity, their dignity.

I found you again in the fifteen-year-old with the black leather vest and the royal blue hair. And there you were a half block further in the shining eyes of the young lesbian who reached over the barricade with a whoop and a high-five for me.

I saw you in a baby's face, a face that might someday be in this parade, straight or gay. I saw you in the supportive smile your sister gave me as we walked shoulder to shoulder. You were there in the smile of the young guy who gently kissed my hand.

I saw you in the tears of a sad young woman as she stood crying in the arms of her lover. You were in the look of delighted recognition from one of your friends. I saw you in the roses that someone passed out to us.

There you were among the shirtless young fellows waving from the windows and the three terrific men who held up "10" signs for us as we passed. That was probably the only perfect score most of us parents will ever get.

I saw you in the faces of the middle aged lesbians pressed against the barricades flashing thumbs up for us. I saw you in the deliciously funny drag queens and the serious care-givers pushing people in wheelchairs.

Then with great joy, I saw *you* burst out of the crowd in your lavender tee-shirt. There we were, you, your sister and I, hugging and laughing and celebrating.

Yes, I found you at the parade. You are my gay child—yesterday, today and tomorrow, old and young, serious and happy. And I love you.

Amazon Mama

Jyl Safier

My Amazon Mama
Keeps her back straight
but nothing else
She can scream like a Banshee
silent when need be
she wears taboo tattoos
under business suits
She knows the ways of the land
can unseat any man
does not flinch from pain
nor live her life tame

My Amazon Mama
taught me how to fight
and be polite
Live without fear
know a woman's care

My Amazon Mama
raised me in a tribe of broad-
   hipped, honey-lipped
leather ladies
big-breasts, tough-skin and
   loud-mouths

who worship the serpent and
   love the hunt
read the stars
know the healing arts

My Amazon Mama taught
   me well
Speak Truth
Do Not Run
Know Your Strength
look directly into the barrel
   of a gun
Woman Warrior
or
WitchBitch
through every age
you face their rage
burned raped
crushed or stoned
you refuse to subdue
your Amazon spirit
And Mama because of you
I am Amazon Warrior too.

Melissa Pinol (left) and her brother, Grant.
Photo: David Elfstone Kalins

Back to the Bear World

for my brother

Melissa Pinol

I turned thirty-eight this year, the same age my brother Grant was when he died. On the anniversary of my brother's passing, I did a meditation. I went back in time in my mind to an important, happy period of my life, to honor Grant and draw the strength and inspiration of that time forward into the present. The year I journeyed to was 1968. In my vision, I was eight years old again and my strange, funny, creative brother was fourteen:

> High on a hill outside of Santa Barbara,
> Away from the prying ears of our parents,
> away from the eyes that speak of disapproval
> My brother and I have met for a Sharing
> in the shade of a fruit tree
> We speak about the Bear World.

My memories of my brother are very clear. We were two souls surrounded by a sea of strangers who thought *we* were strange. The first thing that united us was our awareness of being different—he was different in his own way, I was different in mine, but there were some ways in which we were different together. Throughout my childhood there was only one person who was anything like me. My sister Anna and I didn't understand each other, but Grant's imagination and energy drew me like a magnet. Our parents tried to keep us apart, worried that he would influence me to be myself and not walk down the road they had picked for me. I think they had already given up on him.

My parents reacted to my relationship with my brother with suspicion and a bit of fear, as if they expected us to be plotting some conspiracy against the authority structure of the household. In a way we were, because we continuously validated in each other the things they tried so hard to invalidate. At the very least, they sus-

pected us of being up to "something weird" when we were together. "Weird" seemed to be anything outside of my mother's
conservative Southern standards. As a result, our parents disapproved of us interacting with one another unless we were super-
vised and censured. Though we were supposed to keep to our
separate parts of the house, we still managed to sneak out regularly, meeting in a far corner of the yard or in the hilly remnant
of an avocado orchard across the street. On rainy days we would
sometimes meet in the garage. Grant and I had a kind of sixth
sense between us, and we managed to arrange these meetings with
a minimum of talk and planning. Often, we would just find ourselves going to a particular place, and the other one would be there
waiting. There, hidden away from parental eyes and ears, we
would come together to share realities and confirm each other's
uniqueness.

Once we were together, my brother and I opened our imagina-
tions and let them run wild. We created stories and songs, drew
funny, fantastic pictures, and made magical little objects to share.
Together, we played hunters in the Ice Age, sought out the Faerie
realms, and spoke of Other Realities. We often speculated about
what it would have been like to live in an ancient civilization (the
Ancient Egyptians and Incas were our favorites), and tried to
reconstruct daily life in those times with props we had made or
found around the house. There were sometimes unpleasant repercussions from our play. I was too young to understand why our
parents made such a big fuss and punished Grant for sneaking an
old curtain out of the Goodwill box and draping it around him
like a robe ("in front of your little sister even!") when we were playing Ancient Times. I remember hearing the word "effeminate" used
for the first time, and sensing the terrible disapproval that hung
over him like a shroud.

Back home, separated again, we went on with our rather dreary,
regimented lives. Each time she discovered we had been together
my mother sighed and tried to "normalize" me again, bringing me
Barbie dolls and encouraging me to "be more ladylike" at the age
of nine. To her dismay, I turned Barbie into a Cavewoman with
scraps of fake fur and a tiny spear I had made. When my brother
saw "Cave Barbie," he almost fell over laughing. Never giving up

her attempts at indoctrination, my mother tried enrolling me in "suitable activities" and limiting my access to certain fairy tales, imaginative television shows, or anything else she deemed "weird." I think she was afraid that Grant had somehow "messed up" my sexual orientation. Though I turned out heterosexual, I was always androgynous and not much interested in the traditional feminine role.

Later, Grant and I stole out again to meet on a nearby hill, where we spent the afternoon talking about time travel and the possibility of life on other planets. We made up an imaginary world populated by sentient Teddy Bears with Egyptian names, where the males could wear "robes," the females could wear pants, and either gender could rule or do anything else they wanted. We returned to our special world again and again. I still return to it, sometimes, in my dreams.

My brother and I accepted each other and supported in each other the right to be who we were. In my parents' eyes, something had to be done. When I was ten and he was sixteen, Grant disappeared from my life. I was not told why. Many years later, my parents tried to excuse themselves by explaining that they had found out that he was a "homo," and was involved in unnamed "weird spiritual practices," and "had problems" which they did not want to deal with. They had to get him out of the house to keep him from further "influencing" me. (Too late, Mom and Dad: he already influenced me, and I'm a better person for it.)

Heartbroken, I was forbidden to cry or even mention Grant's name. The conditioning was so strong that to this day I still feel some trepidation about using my brother's name in conversation or even in my writing. If the subject came up inadvertently, a stony silence would descend upon the house. For years, my parents tried to act as if Grant had never existed. My feelings of loss were never addressed. When the subject would not completely die, my parents tried another tactic to silence me—inventing lies, telling me "he doesn't want to see you" and "he might try to hurt you." They even implied that he had attempted to kill me because a rake he had hung in the garage had fallen down in my general vicinity. Nothing could have been farther from the truth. It's true Grant had problems. Anyone who had been treated the way he had been would, but it never seemed to occur to my parents that they should be responsible for helping him. Any helpful efforts by others to urge family counseling and reconciliation were seen as insulting interference. It was easier just to throw my brother away.

Now that he was denied readmission to the house and "access" to me, my sensitive brother, never very physically sturdy, was forced to live on the streets and struggle to survive. I later heard that he tried to work during that time as an assistant in an animal hospital, but in the fragile emotional state he was in following my parents' rejection, he found the suffering of the animals hard to bear. Left on his own at sixteen and desperate for love and support, he found himself falling into some bad scenes and bad company. As can be expected, my parents used this information to justify their rejection and judgment.

Back at home my parents continued to play divide and conquer, encouraging my sister Anna and I to co-exist without speaking to one another. For some reason, they seemed to prefer this unnatural arrangement. During this time, my mother also redoubled her efforts to mold me into "a lady" and "a normal person," but I held on to the memory of being myself and being truly alive. Now that Grant was gone, I was determined not to let the gifts he had given me die. I realize now that he had nurtured a magical spark in me that could never be extinguished, a gift of insight and imagination and independent thought. Because of my brother's influence I found the strength to become a poet and a singer and a storyteller, to walk my own spiritual path and never accept a role I was not comfortable with.

Twenty-three long years later, Anna brought me the news that she knew where Grant was, and that he was very ill. She was still somewhat estranged from me due to our parents' machinations, but we realized that we would have to start working out our differences and come together in this crisis. One thing was clear—I needed to get in touch with Grant right away. When we told our parents this terrible news, they reacted to it as if it were a distasteful subject brought up at the dinner table. Judgmental and uncomfortable, I think they were dismayed at the fact that now that I was an adult they could not forbid me to see him. I set off for Los Angeles as fast as I could to meet my brother.

Together again after so many years, Grant and I started where we had left off—trading stories, offering each other support, just being ourselves. I gave him a stuffed Teddy Bear and asked him if he remembered the Bear World. He did. He was pleased that I had survived our severely dysfunctional family with my character and personality intact (he had feared for years that I would believe the lies and break down and let them turn me "into a robot"). We were amazed to discover that we had both gone into helping professions (he was a nurse, I worked with disabled people) and that we had separately become involved in the same religious path, which was positive and not weird at all. Somehow, we had both ended up following the path of the Goddess and honoring the Earth, though we had arrived there in different ways. My brother shared that he had had several false starts in less positive spiritual traditions, which he now regretted.

Together, we were able to attend our sister's wedding and begin for me the process of healing both relationships. We visited Disneyland, had several visits and many long phone conversations, and then his illness began to gain the upper hand and he began to weaken. I had my dear brother for one more year before he died and was taken away from me again, this time forever. During the last few months of his life, when he was hospitalized and fading, he tried to communicate his last wishes to me. At one point he grasped my hand and asked me to do a memorial service for him when he was gone, because I am a Priestess. He had not thought to put this in his will, and he was too sick and incoherent at that time to think about trying to change things. Grant's wishes on this subject were met with a lot of opposition. Surprisingly, it was not our family that objected, but an elderly individual who had befriended him during the time he had been alone. Grant's friend had supported him during his illness and considered himself to be an adopted father. Because of his strong Jewish beliefs, he was clearly uncomfortable with our Wiccan practices.

During the last month of my brother's life, I broke my femur and was completely incapacitated for a while. I managed to talk to him on the phone several times, but was unable to go down to Los Angeles to visit him one last time with other members of the family. I felt terrible. Belatedly ridden with guilt, my parents visited his bedside near the end and tried to be supportive, but the judgment continued in subtle and not-so-subtle ways. During my last visit I saw my mother go into the bathroom and compulsively scrub her hands after just sitting in the same room with Grant, as if you could somehow contract AIDS through the air. Anna and I were still angry with them—to this day, I blame my brother's final illness on the situation my parents forced him into. Nonetheless, our parents' presence meant a lot to Grant, and that is what was important.

Our last phone conversation was rather strange. Because of my injury and his illness, we were both on heavy painkillers at the time and the conversation had an otherworldly quality to it. I felt that we were communicating in spirit even though we were having difficulty conversing coherently. He died soon afterwards. After his death Grant's elderly friend seized his ashes and did not want to give them up, fearing we were going to do some kind of "evil ritual" with them. My ex-boyfriend David and I fought to honor his wishes, and finally won. The person who offered unexpected support was our father, who managed to get my brother's ashes back and turned them over to me to do a soul release and funeral rite.

We took Grant's ashes high into the Berkeley hills. Because I was recovering from a broken leg and could not walk without crutches, David had to carry me most of the way up the hill on his back. There, in a beautiful, quiet place among the trees and tall grass, we sang and drummed and gave my brother to the wind. We did a ritual for Grant that I think he would have loved. At the end of the ritual, because it felt like the right thing to do, I recited a passage from the Babylonian myth of Ishtar's Descent to the Underworld. The myth is about death, rebirth, and the suffering that often accompanies growth and change. In this passage, the sister-in-law of the Goddess Ishtar speaks of the fact that her brother Tammuz, Ishtar's husband, has gone to the Land of the Dead but will someday return. Belili, Tammuz's sister, speaks of the fear and hope she feels around her brother's departure from this world:

My only brother, bring no harm to me!
On the day when Tammuz comes up to me
When with him the lapis flute and the carnelian ring come up to me
When with him the wailing men and the wailing women come up to me
May the dead rise and smell the incense.

(from The Ancient Near East, v.1, ed. James B. Prichard.
Princeton University Press, 1958)

Reading this, I felt a chill pass through my body and soul and I knew that my brother was with us and that I would be reunited with him again someday. Surprisingly, my father chose to come along for the ritual, though he did not participate. My mother stayed at home.

When Grant died, I think my parents felt some grief, but they still had the audacity to say, "It's for the best. He really messed up his life." I disagree. The world suffered a loss when my brother died. The stories were silenced. The playfulness ended, and never, ever again have I met anyone who was so much like me. Though I will not see him again in this life, the creativity and individuality he nurtured is with me still and part of him lives on in my songs and the stories I tell.

Acceptance

Elizabeth Vickery

My grandson used to be my granddaughter. It is at his suggestion that, at age 82, I write about my acceptance of the problems, developments, and changes of the beautiful baby whom I saw only minutes after she was born.

Acceptance can begin early in life. I was about sixteen when my mother brought home Radclyffe Hall's *The Well of Loneliness* for me to read. I had seen the picture of her in the *Literary Digest* and had tried to figure out if she was a man or a woman. My reaction to the book was sympathy for all the suffering the girl had endured. I thought her novel must have been at least somewhat autobiographical. My mother and I discussed her problems and feelings just as we had discussed *Candide* after I read that book.

Over the years I had talked to my aunt (my mother's sister) also, about all sorts of things. My mother's approach was mainly academic. My aunt's approach was more "down to earth." Between them, I learned a lot about understanding people, male and female.

Acceptance comes more easily when taught early. It also comes from being aware of the problems, changes and happenings over the years to someone you love—to children or grandchildren, for instance. It can be handed down from generation to generation. My mother was born in 1888. I was born in 1915, my daughter in 1942, and my grandson in 1960. When my grandson first came out to her mother, her response was, "Aren't you the person I loved five minutes ago before I knew you were gay?" I was very proud of her for that.

Several years ago my granddaughter, which she was at that time, asked me to go with her to a gay bar. I was probably the only straight person there. We danced together as we always had around home. I liked the women who were her particular friends. I still correspond with one of them once or twice a year.

Humor can be a great help in acceptance, the humor of both people. When my grandson came to visit, sporting a beard, for a day or two it was a little strange, but the personality and voice were very familiar. Two incidents made it much easier. I ran into friends at a restaurant and introduced my grandson. When we got outdoors, he said with a big grin, "Congratulations, Grandma!" "What for?" He replied, "You only called me 'she' twice."

We were in a meat market and the lady waiting on him turned to me as if to say she'd be right with me and I said, "I'm with her." She looked at my grandson with an odd look, clearly meaning "Is that old lady wacko? Can't she see you're a man?" He and I managed to keep our faces straight until we got outside, where we became convulsed with laughter. It was especially therapeutic to us both because we both could see the humor in the situation and the knowing look she gave him. Acceptance can be easy and/or difficult, but as my mother used to say, "You can't help people by turning your back on them." You can learn to understand, as well as to love, them.

Uncomfortable

Duncan Zenobia Saffir

When I go to a bar with my brother
he tells everyone who says hello
to me, "This is my straight brother."

He says he doesn't want me to be
uncomfortable

Truth is he hates it
when anyone flirts with me
instead of him.

III

EXPANDING OUR WORLD

Rhea Murray and Bruce Murray.
Photo: "The Studio"—Jeff Richardson, Seymour, IN

Ms Razz-ma-tazz

Rhea Murray

Viewing myself in the bathroom mirror, I determine that I shouldn't have to apply much blush to my cheeks, considering how flushed they are with excitement tonight.

I simply cannot wait to wear that short, tight, red sequined dress. I have always wanted to wear a dress like that! I love how it dances with red fire every time I move! And, oh girl, can you believe it is a size nine? I never thought I'd see size nine again. I have literally danced 40 pounds off my hips and ass on the Connections' dance floor.

Connections is the gay dance complex in Louisville, Kentucky, about 45 miles from our small town in Indiana. I sponsor my underage gay son there every Saturday night. I dance while my son socializes.

I will never forget the first time I took Bruce to Connections for his eighteenth birthday. The place was packed. We decided that we would first watch the drag show before we danced. We sat up front and center with some of our friends.

Hurricane Summers, their featured drag queen, emceed the show. She was noted for her biting humor and shredding tongue. Well, that famous tongue decided to stop at our table and initiate us to its sting.

Suddenly, our table was flooded in spotlight. She looked at my son coyly and asked what he was doing there. He threw his arm around my shoulder and proudly exclaimed, "I'm here with my mom!"

After almost swallowing her microphone, in true Hurricane form, she belted out, "You brought your fucking mom to a gay bar. You brought your fucking mom!"

The room exploded with laughter. The spotlight shone on us as a thousand eyes filled the black void. They were all on me.

Hurricane proceeded to tease me unmercifully about my ample bosom. Then she stuck the microphone in my face and with a smirk queried, "So, Mom, tell me what you think about all of this?"

"About what?"

"Geeeesh! Talk about the Queen of De—ni—al. You have a man standing in front of you wearing a fuckin' dress!"

"Oh, that! Well, that's an everyday occurrence in *my* house!"

In that moment, Hurricane experienced a first. She was actually speechless. Her famous wagging tongue was frozen to the roof of her blustering mouth. If I thought the room had exploded in laughter before, I realized that it was only a popcorn fart compared to the nuclear explosion that was taking place now.

When it began to die out, a voice rang out, "She really told you, Hurricane!"

And the laughter exploded once again.

This snapped Hurricane out of her frozen stupor. She had the look of battle on her face. Once again, she shoved the microphone in front of me.

"So tell me, what does Daddy dearest think about this?"

"Why don't you ask him?" I pointed to my burly husband Butch, who was sitting at the table next to me with a teen-age girl he had sponsored. She was wearing a white tee-shirt with "BISEXUAL" emblazoned across her chest in bold, black letters.

Once again, we were surrounded by wild laughter that matched ours as Hurricane stormed off, muttering underneath her breath.

There is much more laughter in my life because of this journey I am taking with my gay son, a journey that began with tears, fear and ignorance. Little did I know the radically different course my life would take when my thirteen-year-old son sobbed, "Oh god, Mom, I'm gay!" Little did we both know that this emotional utterance would begin the first leg of our incredible, fascinating adventure together.

I encouraged my son to embrace himself and his sexuality, and as I watched his amazing progress, I was encouraged to embrace my own sexuality.

I learned to let go of what others thought. I began to take action based on my own values. How freeing that is to the soul: to no longer be enslaved by what others think. I grew up hearing the daily mantra, "What will the neighbors say?" Now I only listen to the lady in the mirror who is now applying Erotic Red to her lips. She speaks my truth.

My life is now exploding like the laughter in that room that first night in Connections. This high school drop-out, who was conditioned to be only a mother and a wife, began going to college full-time. I feel immense pride in my 4.0 grade point average. This small town woman who was afraid to drive past her city limits alone, now drives to Chicago or Washington, D.C. on a whim. And I have danced in many gay bars across the nation with loved ones and friends, as I travel to tell our story on many college campuses.

By witnessing my son's courage to speak and live his truth, I have found the courage to speak and live mine. His revelation rescued me from being a soulless clone of June Cleaver.

I decide that I need big hair tonight to go with my razzle dazzle red dress. I smile as I bend over to brush my long hair forward, to give it that much needed glamor volume.

I remember going to the movie premiere of *Stonewall* in Washington, D.C. and actually overhearing a group of men arguing over whether I was a woman or a man in drag.

I worried how my son felt about my new image.

"Puhleeze, Mom," Bruce said. "I would have done anything to get you out of those ugly nylon suits and Ked shoes! And promise me you will never go back to being a pinched-faced Presbyterian again!" He picked me up, twirled me around and threw me through the air.

"Angel Toss!" he yelled.

Angel is his term of endearment for me because he believes I rescued him from a life of despair. I not only accept him, I celebrate him! And now he celebrates me!

After applying my finishing touches, I am ready to make my grand entrance for my two special fellows, Butch and Bruce. It is New Year's Eve and we are going to Connections to dance the New Year in!

"Fellas, ready or not! Here comes Ms Razz-ma-tazz!"

The Pride of a Lion

James M. Pines

When my son came out to me I soon discovered that a lot of people hate homosexuals. I'd known that all along, I guess, but hadn't thought much about it. The full impact of our society's pervasive homophobia becomes apparent only when it affects someone important to you.

Although I went through the usual emotions, one particularly dominated my responses. The fierceness and violence of it astonished me. The way I had always imagined an angry lion, for example, defending cubs against the hunter. I found myself enraged that some people might attack my son, verbally or even physically, for something as private and unobjectionable as his sexual orientation.

Although I continue to mask my rage most of the time, I consider my fierce reaction to be the essence of what masculinity used to mean. Defending your gay child is far tougher, consistent with, and appropriate to being a "real man" than lamenting his tilt away from heterosexuality.

I don't usually worry about my feelings and responses being masculine enough. I'm more concerned that they be human. However, I mention this reaction to my son's coming out because it may help some fathers whose responses are still tied up with the old masculinity myths. Fighting for your gay children is far more "macho" than ignoring them or throwing them out of the house. If you don't turn your back on friends, as "real men" don't, you certainly shouldn't be turning it on your children!

To let down your gay male or lesbian child violates the most natural, fundamental, and intense human attachment any parent can have. As we became more civilized, we began to call it love, but that word just approximates a complex feeling that originated deep in our evolutionary past. Discovering my son's sexual orientation put me in touch with that feeling as nothing else had before.

I sometimes get impatient in support groups and other conversations with parents; there's often too much sophisticated analysis of subtle feelings and self-indulgent wallowing in the grieving process. Too many parents grapple with their ambivalence about homosexual orientation and practices and struggle slowly toward understanding and "acceptance."

All of this may be useful and essential, but neglects a crucial point that comes before everything else. Your child is your child, no matter what, and neither sexual orientation nor anything else changes that. When it comes to acceptance, there's nothing to be subtle or sorry about. Get in touch with the feelings you had when you became a parent. Stop moaning and start being a lion!

That's the "natural," "normal," and "manly" thing to do!

High Tea

Smith College, 1946

Virginia Chase Sutton

Twin china pots on ecru crochet
differ only by a faded rosebud's
partial unfurling. A story I've heard
all my life: aging silver teaspoons

monogrammed with someone else's
initials; heavy cream perfect
in a cut glass pitcher. My parents
have come to tea just days after

their elopement. A woman
in a beret holds the thin saucer
and bone china cup while the other
woman directs a pale stream into the delicate

shell. It's *Royal Doulton*, the set safe
now in my china closet, patterned in lazy
fall gardens trellising up and over
each spout. *They are lovers*, my mother

whispers, loving this unfolding
of a family secret. I can explain
the rest of the day by heart, how he begins
to watch them while trying to remember

the precise rehearsal of crystalled sugar,
the proper grasp of silver tongs. *Black currant,
jasmine, oolong,* he mouths the litany
of tea leaves. Trays of sandwiches fan

into pinwheels. How well Aunt Mary
knows the flowered taste of her lover's
mouth, the twist of her tongue sampling
each glittering bite. Eleanor recites

in Latin, in Greek. Bishop's hats,
madelines, strawberries in eddies
of chocolate. He can't decide. Eleanor
smiles at my mother, fills his plate

with shortbread and scones, dips
a well of clotted cream and cherry jam,
slides it to his astonished hands.
Can you picture them in bed, he wonders.

One candied violet eases to his lips.
We name our daughters for them,
my mother explains. I know she slides
her pretty tongue between his teeth,

licks the sweetness gathering
in his mouth. This afternoon they like
the balance of women, the tiered
racks of silver tea things.

The poem is about my great-aunt Mary Ellen Chase, and her long-term lover Eleanor Duckett. Aunt Mary was a well-known writer in the forties, and taught for nearly thirty years in the English Department of Smith College. Their relationship was well known in the family and at Smith. They are buried side by side in the family graveyard in Maine.

The World Needs All Kinds of Music

Dean L. Rosen

My son Adam is lucky. At 18 he knows who he is, where he fits in and where he's going with his life. His identity as a gay youth is clear; he is totally accepted. This shouldn't be such a remarkable achievement. But it is, even in the more enlightened 1990s. His life today is quite rich and varied.

I had no idea Adam's life would turn out so successfully. I pretty much always knew he was gay—that was never a surprise. And I never thought it was anything tragic or abhorrent. But I worried that his life would be harder for him and it hurt me to see this delightful, social little boy become withdrawn and isolated as he experienced rejection for not acting like a "typical" little boy.

Adam was gender "atypical." He played with dolls and liked to play house with the other girls in preschool and kindergarten. He never liked sports and rough housing.

I remember foolishly asking his kindergarten teacher to encourage Adam to play with other boys more, thinking this might help socialize him better. Wisely, Mrs. DiMartino told me that "Adam marches to the beat of a different drummer, and the world needs all kinds of music." I never forgot those kind and knowing words. They often comforted me as I struggled to understand this very "different" little boy. And in the end, I have learned much from Adam on the importance of being oneself—one's true self—and not denying yourself in order to fit in. For this alone I have enormous respect for him—more than he probably realizes.

I watched in much pain as Adam struggled with the social rejections of grade school and junior high. He withdrew into a world of imagination, music and learning. Adam loved reading and would get intensely interested in some subject, pursuing it in great depth. He was especially gifted musically and could spend hours listening to Beethoven, Handel, and Mozart. He would follow along reading the scores as he listened to his music. He was attracted to requiems, oratorios, and operas.

Adam acted indifferent to the other kids, but I knew he hurt inside. At times his bitterness and anger would explode on the safe target of his family. He always wanted us to go to school and make the kids stop their teasing and rejection. We tried to protect him from the worst physical torments, but I really felt helpless.

While I couldn't help him with his social failures, I could help him develop his talents and strengths. By age eight Adam and I were going to the symphony together. He actually took me; he picked out the programs he wanted to hear and dragged me along. He could be quite insistent and demanding, but I didn't want to deny him these experiences. He had definite tastes, and it was hard to expose him to something he didn't think up first. At the time he developed his passion for opera, I tried to get him exposed to more contemporary musical theater since I could see no future for him composing eighteenth-century operas. I knew his taste for the outlandish and camp. I made sure we saw *Priscilla, Queen of the Desert* and *La Cage Aux Folles*. I also took him to a production of *A Chorus Line*, a seminal event in his artistic development. Years before he came out to us as gay, I was aware of his gay sensitivity and made sure he was exposed to positive images in the movies and theater.

When Adam came out to us at age 16 he was on fire to learn everything he could about gay life and gay history. We generously supported his growing library of books on the subject. And we took him to our public library, even before he came out to us, letting him check out every book he wanted on these "taboo" topics. We attended the local gay men's chorus, gay performance artists who tell their stories in monologues, and plays and musicals in the new gay theater. There is now a gay film festival in St. Louis where Adam can go with his friends from the gay youth group to see their lives and their culture depicted on the screen.

Adam does get support from all his family—brother, sister, mom, grandparents, aunts and uncles. This support gives him that extra boost to go out there in the world and fight for his rightful place. Sadly, most of his gay friends are not getting such unqualified support. Hopefully, their parents will come around to accepting what initially is unacceptable. Some of his friends have been kicked out of their homes or fear they will be if they come out.

They must sneak and hide their identity, not telling their parents of the gay youth group they attend each week. I feel that I am the lucky one because I get to share in Adam's life, and an exciting life it is.

My son is young, gay, and healthy. Parents need to recognize and accept this aspect of their child's identity and nurture it socially, spiritually, and culturally. The process ideally should start way before a child comes out with his or her orientation. Children need to learn there are many ways to be in this world. We must do much more than merely accept. We have to validate and cherish all of our gay children and help them grow into this identity and this culture. It's a new journey for our children and for us. They shouldn't have to take the journey all by themselves. And if we are lucky they will share their lives with us.

What Is the Answer? What Is the Question?

for Minnie Bruce Pratt

Kim Roberts

History is much too long;
geography goes too far.

A young girl imagines herself
into a graying, dog-eared photograph:
the slim lines of a long skirt
drop just above the pointy shoes
with the line of pearl buttons,
ten per shoe, slightly off-center.

Those buttons toil up a narrow trail
at the beginning of an uncertain journey
over the literal foothills;
they will not risk the heights
to the garters, the thick reinforced corset
that must be there, underneath
all those intricate layers.

One long-fingered hand drapes
down a thigh while the other
reaches up to a large feathered hat,
the shadow of which partially obscures

a rather plain face. Time
becomes tedious; distance moves
just out of reach. That face
could be hers: the chin, the cheekbones.
"Who is she?" she asks the grandmother.
Those shoes, those hands.

"That is your Great-Uncle Eli.
he always dressed in women's clothes."
Data is matter-of-fact—
cumulative, stored up in layers,
a glimpse of lace, a pocket and seam,
elemental as the air around us—
we barely know it's there.

Pat Mayne (left) and Jennifer Harris.
Photo: Audrey Ellis

The Way Our Lives Are Interwoven

for my cousin, Pat Mayne

Jennifer Harris

I was born on your 19th birthday.

Throughout my childhood you sent me unexpected gifts that sparked my imagination: a small orange, cream and gold tapestry purse hanging on a jet black cord which made me think of India; a paper maché pin of a woman in a smart dress and hat that looked like she belonged in Paris. I often wondered about far away places and decided at age six that I would see them someday.

At family gatherings you came with a rabbit puppet named Leonard and delighted me with your gift of story-telling. With a skilled imagination you bridged the gap between adult and child, and in time, you opened my eyes to a whole new world of books and learning that has become a part of the core of my being.

On weekend trips to Vancouver you took me to the Art Gallery, Gastown, Granville Island, Lonsdale Quay, and Stanley Park. We hiked up Grouse Mountain and walked English Bay. One New Year's Eve we went to First Night and listened to all kinds of music. The next morning we watched the Polar Bear Swim from your apartment window. We window shopped, people watched, saw improvisational theatre, ate out and went to movies. Thanks to you I learned my way around the city, I know how to read transportation schedules and discern north and south.

Most importantly, you created space where it was safe to talk about absolutely anything, to trust my perceptions to grow from experience, to heal, and to dream. You have always accepted me, as I am and am not, in the here and now. You are an inspiration and your love has given me the courage to do things I never thought I could.

Leaving home at 17 to be an exchange student in France was one of the most difficult and daring things I have ever done. We talked and wrote for a long time about the pros and cons of going. Most people were focused on the negatives like being home-

73

sick and not being able to graduate with my friends. It was sometimes difficult to talk to people, especially my parents, because they were so emotionally involved and worried about my welfare. I had just been in a serious car accident, and throughout my recovery from broken legs and my struggle to catch up and excel at school, you listened, wrote and remained supportive. You helped me hear the words of my heart and you had faith in me.

The year of my exchange to France, you had moved to England. It felt comforting to have you so close. The trip we did together at the end of my year was transformative. We saw Buckingham Palace, Madame Tussaud's, St. Paul's Cathedral, and the Tower of London. On the train, I comforted you over the loss of a friendship, and as you cried, I realized I was a woman and your equal. We visited Jane Austin's grave and saw family friends that knew our grandparents. I was so young when our grandmother died. I have never been able to completely express how deeply I miss her. You comforted me and set me on a path of healing that I am still learning to walk today.

In Ireland, you picked up the accent so quickly that people asked you what county you were from. I can still picture the streets we walked at dusk while you told me about Barbara Hambly's book, *Those Who Hunt the Night*. I think of those streets and I still feel the chill of vampires. We visited family, saw *Hedda Gabler*, stayed in George Bernard Shaw's home turned hotel, and drove through the breathtaking countryside. We saw the Blarney stone, the Cliffs of Mohur, the U2 wall, and we had quiet times of reflection. I love to think of us visiting pubs, having Guinness, ale or beer while speaking intently or listening to local musicians.

Most of all I remember the cloaks we bought. Yours is black and mine is navy blue. We happened upon them in a store and fell in love. They are a combination of wool and cashmere—durable, water-resistant, warm and incredibly soft and light. They are simple, with deep pockets, an elegant drape, and they pack up into a ball without creasing. Wearing the hood makes me feel like I am in Avalon. Living in separate cities as we do, I like to wear my cloak and think of you wearing yours. They remain a tangible reminder of Ireland and you and a visible symbol of the way our lives are interwoven.

In my favorite picture of you, you are wrapped in your cloak, sitting among the rocks in a field of heather. I carried heather in my wedding bouquet. It was my way of having you close and thanking you. You challenged me to define what feminism meant to me and to really look at marriage with all its sexist and hetero-sexist traditions. I believe I make more informed and inclusive decisions because of you.

Perhaps this is trivial, but I have always loved how you dress. Your clothes speak of comfort, casual style, quality, and always a hint of something different—foreign. Good sturdy shoes that could walk miles; rich colors and textures; warm winter sweaters and a silk scarf; a man's hat that made me think of a detective or spy; a great brooch or ring, and always your silver and bloodstone cuff bracelet. I know you got criticized for not looking "feminine" and I want to thank you for setting such a positive example. You taught me to like my face with and without make up and to appreciate good hygiene and neatness as an act of self love. I have learned that being feminine does not have to mean wearing uncomfortable, ill-fitting, poorly made clothing that is designed primarily to please the male gaze. Good quality does not have to be expensive, and does not date itself quickly. Simplicity has an elegance and style of its own. Most of all, I have learned that your clothes should accent you and enable you to function optimally.

Thank you for your support of my schooling. The freedom to engage in academic debate and social issues helped me to overcome many of my fears of speaking my mind. One summer I bought us both t-shirts. Yours read, "Strong enough for a man but made for a woman," and mine read, "Straight but not narrow." We went to the Pride Parade together. It was an exhilarating, colorful, and loving experience I will never forget.

You have always encouraged me to follow my dreams no matter where they took me and that meant facing other's expectations of me in university. I never knew I was expected to study anything in particular until I decided to major in Women's Studies, History and Sociology. Suddenly, I found myself being asked if those were "real subjects" worthy of academic pursuit. You came to visit me in Toronto. You even attended classes with me. You believed that my academic pursuits were valuable. You believed I could go to graduate school and you encouraged me to write. Even when I opted to postpone grad school indefinitely, and most people said how smart I was to take a break because school is so demanding, you knew about my miscarriage. You knew even as it was happening that I was distancing myself and slipping into denial. You called it by name and then gave me space to shut down. Months later when I could name it myself, you held me as I sobbed my grief. I have yet to meet someone who has never experienced the death of her own baby, to show such compassion and sensitivity. For your depth and love, I thank you from the bottom of my heart.

Now, as I live day to day trying to follow my heart and become the woman and artist I want to be, I am again struck by your influence and your continual loving presence. You challenge me to know and trust myself and to live with truth, integrity, and love. You are my family and my friend. You are my strongest, most knowing guide and I am so glad you are here.

The Perks

Nancy Lamkin Olson

You know, I've always thought that one of the perks of having a gay son is that a mother is able to carry on a conversation similar to the following:

Mom: Did you see the cover of *Vanity Fair* with Matthew McConaughey on it? Is he a lust bunny or what?

Son: Mother, how old are you?

Mom: Well, let me see, dear. My driver's license, which I am certain is erroneous, claims I'm going to be 56 on my next birthday. What's your point exactly?

Son: Matthew McConaughey is younger than I am, you hussy.

Mom: Like you wouldn't "go there" if you could, assuming that your sweetie, Tom, was dead, of course and you were a grieving widower.

Son: Oooooooh, what a combination. Hip *and* Perverted. The phrase "sick puppy" comes to mind. And, for your information, if, God forbid, Tom were to bite the Big One, I'd "go there" with Leonardo DiCaprio, thank you very much.

Now you see, my theory is that this isn't a conversation that most mothers in America probably have with their sons. I mean I have two straight sons and I can't remember when the last time was that I commented about what a hot babe Julia Roberts is, for example.

It has been said, and I think this might be stereotypical, that mothers have a special bond with their male children and that you double it if he happens to be gay. I'm not exactly sure about this because I have an extraordinarily close relationship with my straight sons and like to think I love them all equally. But perhaps it is true that as mothers we do respond more to the runt of the litter, and by runt, I mean the child who has the most difficulty being accepted by mainstream society. It's heartbreaking to know that two of your children can be with their significant others and it's perfectly acceptable for them to hold hands or share a kiss in public. But when my gay son and his life partner are walking down a street, it's very likely that a carload of morons will drive by and shout hateful epithets just because they're walking closely together, side by side. It's actually happened before on Wells Street in Chicago.

The family was walking north heading to Piper's Alley and I had wandered on ahead while window shopping. My son and his partner were walking together and my husband was slightly in front of them. As the carload of homophobes drove by, screaming, "Hey, look at the two faggots!" my son had to say to his father, "Dad, don't say anything, please. Just keep walking."

That's tragic, I think, and ultimately damaging to two very precious gay souls.

So, if a mother and her gay son share a special bond, then so be it. He deserves all the bonds he can get and I, as his mother, happen to love the perks.

Passenger

Shirley Powers

Motorcycle exhaust fumes make it
difficult to concentrate on
sitting erect. Heat rises
from pavement dotted with
sun spots never as bright
as this daughter of Sappho.
This first born Queen of the Road

My Motherly fear registers
on the sleeve of her black
leather jacket. I remind myself
"do not lean to left or right: but
                    balance."
To avoid a spill in this
Gay Freedom Day parade, I hang on
along a route where
local bigots scream "death to queers"
among thousands cheering approval.
Holding her slender waist is
easier than descending to pinnacle caves and yet
more difficult.

No longer does she ride my shoulders
on marches past police barricades
down a dusty road to the Freedom School.
We follow a lavender strip down the middle of Market Street
and we balance
                    on center.

Patricia B. Campbell (left) and Kathryn Campbell Kibler
dancing at Kathryn's wedding.
Photo: Matt, Smith/Wright Photography

Ten Reasons to Be Happy
That Your Daughter Is Bisexual

Patricia B. Campbell

1. Your daughter's date can wear your black velvet gown to the prom.
2. You learn about and read books like Carol Queen's *Exhibitionism for the Shy*, and Susie Bright's *Sexual State of the Union*.
3. You receive lots and lots of admiration and hugs when you march with your daughter at Gay Rights demonstrations.
4. You find some great research assistants to hire at the Women's Center while you wait for your daughter to finish her bisexual support group meeting.
5. You can read *Out* magazine and get to see great pictures of Greg Louganis without having to buy your own subscription.
6. You can say things like, "My daughter is the head of Queers and Associates and is in love with a guy named Mort."
7. You can get your very own account at Good Vibrations, give catalogs to your friends and watch their reactions to a feminist display of dildos.
8. You "get" most of Kate Clinton's jokes—even the one about going where no man has gone before.
9. You realize that it's cool to be half of the oldest, straightest, fastest couple doing the Boston New York AIDS Ride.
10. You have a daughter who is who she is and who helps to make your life wonderful.

Dia de los Muertes:
A Chance to Celebrate a Loved One's Life

Liz Armstrong

My husband Chuck and I lost our youngest son, Jeff, to AIDS in '93. He was 36 years old and oh how we cherish his memory and the ways that he enriched our family. Though we are not Latino, we decided to celebrate our son Jeff's life by observing Dia de los Muertes (Day of the Dead).

Diversity seemed to symbolize Jeff's life. He sought and treasured experiencing diverse people, cultures, and philosophy. His photo collection is filled with all types and ages of people and scenes from trips to Africa, Japan, Israel, South America, Europe, Thailand, and more. Meaningful times in his life included cradling a newborn baby in his arms, playing with his nephews, and cribbage games with his grandmother. Travel treasures ranged from pygmy artifacts to a Matsuda tuxedo. His bookshelves displayed his intense interest in art, religion, poetry, and science. We're reminded of Jeff's love of life and humor by his mardi gras beads, comic art, black satin sheets and tin badge saying "I Want It All."

On November 1, 1996, for Dia de los Muertes, we created an altar for Jeff in his room complete with candles, flowers, photos, and some of his favorite things. I used a pair of his favorite shoes as bookends for travel books from his trips, hung strings of beads from his many trips to New Orleans for Mardi Gras, put out his favorite coffeecake, the bottle of Cristal champagne he had been saving for a special occasion, crystal flutes, a few high tech gadgets that fascinated him and his "I Want It All" pin. We invited two gay couples over, Jeff's favorite friends. We lounged on his water bed and drank champagne as I proposed a toast . . . "To the gay spirits who have playfully and profoundly enriched our world." We laughed and cried over some outrageous memories and stories of Jeff that the altar reminded us of. Later we took the guys to dinner at a neighborhood restaurant. I surprised them with their first look at a tile bearing Jeff's name that we had placed in the new sidewalk for a neighborhood improvement project. The evening was warm, fun, and left me very contented. We repeated the evening with our oldest grandson who loved Jeff. He was so moved that a few nights later he brought his Mexican girlfriend to see the sidewalk and hear about his Uncle Jeff.

Spending this time with his favorite things, happy memories, and merry friends is a very positive and healing way to celebrate the life of a loved one who has given us great joy and inspiration.

In future years we may include others but this night was Jeff's and we felt he was enjoying it with us.

The Kvelling Grandma

Margy Kleinerman

kvell, v. (Yiddish) to be so proud that you are ready to burst and are compelled to tell the world about it.

"Kvell" certainly describes how I feel about my son Brad and his partner Flint. They have been together for eight years, have their own business and are working very hard to succeed.

Brad and Flint had a great desire to be parents. They decided to adopt and after two years of filing applications, meeting with social workers, and getting clearances, they met Raymond and Ricky, 5 and 6 year-old brothers.

It was love at first sight.

The boys had been removed from their parents at birth and had spent their entire lives in foster homes. They were removed from their first foster home by the police and social workers.

At dinner that night, Brad and Flint told us how cute the boys were. The three of us went to The Teacher's Supply and I bought toys, games, and books.

Brad and Flint met the boys at the park for a picnic. They had a wonderful time running, climbing and just being kids. When the social worker wanted to take them back to the foster home they both started to cry. Ricky hid behind a tree, hoping that the social worker wouldn't find him.

Their next get together was a visit to their new home and arrangements were made for a sleep over. Brad and Flint made the boys a calendar and gave them happy face stickers to indicate when the next meeting would be.

Brad and Flint had the boys' room beautifully decorated with large alphabet letters that spelled RICKY and RAYMOND. They bought a toy fire engine and ambulance, both with sirens, stuffed animals, and books. They hung a basketball hoop above the small patio. The four of them played for a few hours, and then went to

McDonald's for dinner. When the boys had to return to the foster home, Raymond was crying so hard that Flint had to get in the back seat to comfort and reassure him that they would be back.

The social worker felt it was too emotionally damaging for the boys (not to mention their prospective daddies) to have to go through this again, so on their next visit they were allowed to stay permanently. Both boys had a duffel bag of mostly worn-out clothing and the beanie baby Dalmatian puppies Brad and Flint had given them on their first meeting. The next day they went to Mervyn's for a complete new wardrobe. They were surprised that they could choose more than one shirt, pants, pajamas, etc.

Soon their individual personalities began to show.

Ricky is affectionate and wants to be kissed and cuddled. Raymond is a little more reserved and does not want to be kissed or even touched very much. After a lovely dinner, which they helped prepare, we were relaxing in the living room. Raymond threw his smurf ball at me. I told him it would cost him a kiss to get the ball back. He decided it wasn't worth it and went downstairs to play with his Legos. Ricky climbed into my lap, cuddled for a little while, kissed me and then asked if he could have the ball. I surrendered it, of course. He immediately ran to the stairs and yelled, "Hey, Raymond, I got the ball back for you." We all collapsed with laughter.

The first night of Chanukah, my daughter Stephanie and I went to Brad, Flint, Raymond and Ricky's home for dinner. The boys had no Jewish education. Brad read them the story of Chanukah. Flint is Catholic, but it was decided that the children would be raised as Jews. They each had their own Menorah and we lit the candles. Of course I bought them a gift for each night. It was the first holiday season for many years that I had little children with whom to celebrate. It was wonderful. Grandma Jane, Flint's mother, also got them each a gift from her to open for the first night.

We also spent Christmas Day together. Here were two boys who came from having no one and nothing to having aunts, uncles, cousins and two doting grandmas. They had a wonderful time opening gifts. Brad and Flint made it very clear that some were share toys, some were personal and did not have to be shared (but it would be nice if they were) and some would be put away for rainy days. They were very appreciative and said, "Cool!" or "I always wanted one of these."

The next day, we met at the nursing home so they could meet Grandpa Joe, my husband who has Alzheimer's. They brought him candy and fed him pieces. They also shared the puppets they had brought to play with in the car. I am not sure how much Joe really understood but when I told him, "These are our grandchildren," he smiled.

Brad and Flint had an open house to introduce the boys to friends and relatives. Many of my friends had not known openly-gay people before, and seemed surprised at how "normal" everything was. The boys were wonderful. They were well behaved, greeted everyone and thanked them for the presents. They were not the least bit shy. My friends were all enchanted with these adorable little boys. Raymond helped himself to a plateful of cookies and then joined some of the other guests on the driveway. Because the daddies are strict about the sweets in their diet, Raymond felt he was getting away with something. He didn't know that the rules were suspended for the day.

March 3 was Ricky's birthday. The day started with birthday cake and hats for his classmates. Then a quiet family dinner with Jane and me. Ricky could not believe that all these presents were for him, and would not have to be shared. As he unwrapped the gifts Raymond kept saying, "That's a good toy for sharing."

After the presents were open, we had birthday cake. Ricky and I may not be genetically related, but he shares my love for anything chocolate and fattening. Ricky said, "It was my birthday when I woke up and it's still my birthday." As far as we know he never had more than a token gift.

Raymond and Ricky seldom, if ever, had stories read to them so it was hard to get them to listen at first. Now they can listen for a good period of time. Both daddies wish Curious George would take a vacation, but when they are asked which story they choose, George wins.

Because the boys had no formal schooling, Raymond was put into kindergarten and Ricky in preschool. Raymond's teacher says that he is catching up rapidly and will do very well in first grade.

Out of the 20 kids in his class, only 2 are living with both their biological parents. Most are living with stepparents, single moms, grandparents, etc. and have no problem with Raymond having two daddies. When one of the children asked him why he had two daddies, he said, "I'm lucky."

The boys first called both Brad and Flint "Daddy" and whoever was out of the room was called "the other Daddy." Now Rick and Raymond call Brad "Daddy" and Flint "Papa."

When Brad was driving them home from school one day, Raymond was chanting, "Papa and Daddy sitting in a tree. K-I-S-S-I-N-G."

The boys are really secure now. The other day the daddies were discussing something about the house and Raymond said, "It's our house too!!"

I have become the typical grandma. I carry their pictures around all the time and I show them at every opportunity. For Chanukah, Brad and Flint gave me a T-shirt that says, "If you are close enough to read this shirt, you are close enough to look at pictures of my grandchildren."

This beautiful family has done so much to enrich my old age. I have much to *kvell* about and I don't hesitate to do so.

The Fault

for Laura and Susan

Sondra Zeidenstein

These two women, lovers,
mothers of newborn
Julian
split the earth
along its fault:

those who trust
that love
surely
as the rush
of milk
will nourish;

and those who'd
narrow
to the sanctioned
jet of semen
who would be allowed
to bear a child.

These two women lovers
drive a canyon
deep as Susan

witching her love
when labor slows
in the terrible night

with tales
of how the moon
draws down the tides
draws down:

wide as Laura
on her hands and knees
opening.

These two women
draw the line
firm as the memory
of curls
in Laura's sweated hair

unambiguous
as Julian's crimson cry

sure as the fit
of lips to nipple.

Let skeptics
rear back
in discomfort.

The blessed
hold up a flower
and smile.

IV

TAKING OUR FAITH SERIOUSLY

Back row (left to right): Wave Starnes and Tom Starnes (Floyd's parents), Celina Gomez (Carlos' mother), Keott Gomez-Starnes. Front row: Floyd Starnes, Carlos Gomez, Dylan Gomez-Starnes (adopted since article). Photo: Crystal Belton of Picture People

A Family's Blessings

Tom Starnes

The Starnes family got together for its annual gathering on Sunday, December 28, 1997. We have been doing this on the Sunday between Christmas and New Year's for almost 40 years now. This year we met at Floyd and Carlos's house.

Floyd and Carlos.

Floyd is our baby, a real charmer from the day in 1960 when he opened his eyes in the old Sibley Hospital that used to sit on North Capitol Street. Everybody has loved Floyd along the way, and he has returned the favor.

On the spring day in 1981 when he told me he was gay, it came as no great surprise. Handsome as he could be, with girls dogging his every step, Floyd never really dated—aside from a prom or two.

Yet I also felt a feeling in the pit of my stomach that I have never been able to tag. Was it fear about what this might do to the father-son relationship that meant so much to me?

I hurt for him. That surely was a part of what I felt that day. How hard it must have been, how much courage it must have taken to say it—to his dad—whom, he must have felt, might be repulsed by the whole notion of having a gay son.

I hurt because guys like me had been telling and laughing at "queer" jokes for years. It pained me to think that my son would be the butt of such stories, though, as he later told me, he had already lived through years of ridicule, quite often at the hands of his male school teachers.

But what I have cherished from that day—other than Floyd's courage and honesty to claim who he is—is that within our family, he chose to tell me first. I treasure that gift.

The next day I told a colleague at work, and she said, "Just wait until you get to the 'guess who's coming to dinner' stage."

That day came. And Carlos is now one of the family.

He's a wonderful companion. He talks like Desi Arnaz. He is

a gourmet cook, which has helped him close more than just a bit of the gap between him and Granny Trout, my wife's mother. (Anyone who can make good gravy must have something going for him.)

Keott is one of the family, too. He is the 9-year-old boy that Floyd and Carlos took in at age 3 and adopted just last year. Floyd and Carlos are wonderful parents. It is nothing short of amazing to watch Keott's development. To see a terrorized, apprehensive child move along the way toward becoming an open, loving, trusting child is a sight to behold.

So, the Starnes clan gathered at Floyd, Carlos and Keott's house for our annual Christmas/New Year's family reunion.

There are a bunch of us. I was one of eight brothers and sisters to begin with: five girls and three boys. Benton was gone before we started getting together. Elizabeth died in 1976, and Lucille died last year. Joining the five of us who are left are about 50 or so children, grandchildren, great-grandchildren and assorted in-laws.

There was a time when not all of the family would have come. One relative, who is no longer alive, thought it was "wrong" to be gay; another declined to attend a celebration that Floyd and Carlos had to mark the fifth anniversary of their relationship.

But there we all were, ranging in ages from 4 months to 72 years, exchanging gifts, eating wonderful food, watching football, reminiscing, asking my niece Wendy when her baby is due and sharing health inventories. Just the normal stuff of which family holiday gatherings are made.

We are also a family that takes its faith seriously. Although we have moved on from the revivals and hell-fire preaching that my generation was reared on, we are still trying, as best we all can, to serve faithfully the God of our understanding. So our Christmas gatherings are not just family reunions scheduled around a national holiday. They are also times when we come together and remember how blessed we have been as a family, and how fortunate we are to have each other.

We did that on Sunday—and we were doing nothing less than upholding the strong family values of love and acceptance that were so high on Daddy and Mama Starnes's list of priorities.

The Heart of a Flower

Carole and Richard L. Fowler

Did you ever know anyone who believed in a flower? I mean someone who trusted in its growth, life, truth, and beauty? And then, did you ever know anyone who received that truth and beauty as a gift so wondrous, it seemed a miracle? We did.

In 1975, at age 12, our son Scott, developed a green thumb.

Scott was born into a lineage of farmers. He was the 10th generation to live in the same town where his father, grandfather, and great-grandfathers were born, lived, worked and died. They began settling in Westfield, Massachusetts in 1669.

Planting was inherent in Scott's nature. He relished becoming a carrot farmer along with his dad, brothers and grandfather; yet his love of the soil focused on growing flowers.

After school, Scott would walk to the newly opened nursery in town and ask to help out with odd jobs. Two young women owned the shop and liked Scott's persistent, pleasant manner. They allowed Scott to water, carry plants from one area of the shop to another, even go on purchasing trips to the flower market. Within a short time, Scott wove his way into their hearts and the hearts of many customers.

Scott quickly learned both the common and Latin names of the plants. He learned the basic nutrient requirements. He took pride in pronouncing the long, complicated names of many tropical plants, including the orchid family. In a year's time, orchids became his "specialty." In 1976, he joined the American Orchid Society, becoming one of the youngest members. At that time, he ordered a type of cattleya orchid to grow as a challenge. The flower was known to be exquisitely beautiful. This was his first orchid.

Scott completed private school at the age of 18, and entered college at Massachusetts College of Art in Boston. He carried his plants from home to his apartments.

After college, Scott moved to various cities and countries, pursuing educational and vocational interests. During this transitional period, the orchids also experienced constant change, often returning home to the family's care.

All the orchids remained healthy and green, but this first orchid did not flower.

"Scott," we said, "this orchid never blooms. Why do you care about this plant?"

"Someday my orchid will bloom," he said. "Have faith. When it is time, the orchid will produce its flowers in all their splendor. Keep fertilizing. Keep watering. Have patience."

Thirteen years later, at age 26, Scott moved from Ibiza, Spain to San Francisco, California. His entire plant collection traveled with him including his first orchid.

"Why are you even bothering with this orchid?" we asked again. "It will not bloom."

He picked up the orchid, hugged it with love, and said in a determined voice, "Believe me it will bloom. Remember, give it its own time."

In the summer of 1992, the AIDS virus that Scott carried in his body raised havoc with his immune system. He became gravely ill. His physical strength weakened while his spiritual strength grew. Now was the time for those who loved Scott to surround him with harmony and nurturing. Scott directed us to carefully attend to his orchid plants, including the "reluctant" orchid.

A week before Scott died, his partner noticed a bud had formed on the reluctant orchid plant. Amazed and thrilled, he immediately told Scott.

Even though Scott was blind, he smiled peacefully and said, "I knew it was important to have faith and trust and patience."

"It has been 16 years since we began caring for this orchid," we said. "What is it going to look like?"

"Oh, it will be so gorgeous, so incredible, so beautiful!" Scott exclaimed. "The colors are deep and rich. Brilliant!"

His hands formed the shape of a flower as he described every detail: deep purple with variegated magenta, yellow and white center, ruffled edge.

Each day the bud increased in fullness. A week later, on a Thursday morning, the flower began to unfold. We ran to Scott's bedside once we realized the orchid was in the onset of bloom. We were anxiously reporting the news faster than the words would form. Near death, Scott managed a warm smile.

"I knew. I really did know my orchid would flower someday when it was the right time." Then he added, "I had faith."

That evening at 11:22 p.m., as Scott breathed his final breath, as we surrounded him with love, his orchid unfolded its bloom to the fullest, most magnificent flower one could behold, exactly as Scott had described its glory.

In God's wondrous grace, they joined together in eternal life.

Thursday, October 22, 1992
Printed in a publication the same day from "A Flower Does Not Talk" by Z. Shibayama, Tuttle, Tokyo, 1070

> "Silent a flower blooms,
> In silence it falls away:
> Yet here now, at this moment, at this place,
> the whole of the flower, the whole of
> the world is blooming.
> This is the talk of the flower, the truth of
> the blossom,
> The glory of eternal life is fully shining here."

Seder Night in the Melting Pot

Dvora Luz

In Israel there is not only unrest, political feuds and terrorism; there are also miracles. Let me tell you about the Seder night I attended this year on the eve of Passover, and you tell me if it is not at least close to a miracle in these days of fanaticism, narrow-mindedness and bigotry.

Passover is the Jewish holiday that celebrates the deliverance of the Sons of Israel from slavery—from being second-class citizens.

My son Ami and his life-partner Pat decided to have the Seder in their apartment and invited their mothers and siblings with their loved ones. After all, where is it written that the Seder must always be held at the home of the elders of the family?

Three generations were represented at the Seder, originating from different countries and different cultures:

Grandmother Rose, Pat's mother, was born in India and came to Israel as a little girl. Later she married a Yemenite Jew with whom she had ten children. I was born in Czechoslovakia, and came to Israel as a refugee at the beginning of World War II. The third grandmother, Tamara, is a new immigrant from the Ukraine. She came to the Seder with her daughter Irina who is married to one of Pat's brothers.

The middle generation, all born in Israel, are the descendants of the Indian-Yemenite couple, of Czech parents, and of Moroccan, Russian, Polish families.

The third generation, our grandchildren, couldn't care less where their grandparents had immigrated from, or whether their fathers or uncles were straight or gay, religious or free thinking.

Songs were sung, some according to the Yemenite tradition, others in the way they were sung by our great-grandparents in Europe. The food, too, was a medley of tastes and traditions:

First we had Tamara's "borscht" (a Russian cabbage soup), then some Polish style gefilte fish and my famous chicken soup with the little matzo dumplings. Ami and Pat prepared a pot roast and chicken and Pat's sisters brought Indian rice, chutney and various salads. After the traditional hard-boiled eggs, bitter herbs and charoses (a mixture of apples, dates and ground almonds) eaten during prayers, and after the huge dinner that followed, not even the greediest could do justice to the dessert.

However, the focus was neither on the variegated menu nor the traditional aspect of the evening. The focus was on the holiday spirit, the feeling of togetherness and love.

Once you cross the bridge over prejudice, ignorance and ill will, opening your eyes, ears and hearts to the other, you don't see the differences any more and are free to love your fellow man for who he really is.

The Wedding

Norman Diamond

After the ceremony ended, I drew the Rabbi aside to a quiet place under a tree. I asked him how he came to the decision to perform the wedding. I said, "Very few Rabbis would risk the disapproval of those who feel that the Bible prohibits a marriage between two lesbians." Rabbi Joey answered my question in this way.

"Norman, in the years that Barbara and Beth have been active members of our Congregation, I have gotten to know them both well. The spirit of Judaism is an important part of their life. They are good observant Jews. To me Judaism is a religion of love. It is big enough to gather all Jews into its arms. I am sure I speak for God by blessing the union of two honorable, courageous and loving women."

His eyes shone like stars as he turned and left me under the tree. His bright white robe seemed like angel's wings.

Almost 3 years ago my grandson Noah was born to Barbara. My wife and I went to Portland, Oregon and shared in the joy of the naming of Noah by Rabbi Joey. When Barbara had come out to me twelve years ago, I gave up the dream that some day she'd get married and have children. Reality became better than my dream, except that she had Noah before they thought of getting married.

My eyes turned toward the dancers whirling to the music of the Hora. Noah and his two cousins, and the two daughters of Barbara's dearest friend from Great Neck, danced the Hora looking like romping puppies.

The beginning of the ceremony flashed in my mind. Rabbi Joey stood under the Chuppah, his eyes fixed on the wedding couple. Hand in hand, they walked to face the Rabbi, then turned—their eyes fixed on each other, faces full of love. Time stopped at that moment. The love between them was like a powerful magnet, its force reaching out joining everyone together in one loving spirit.

No one breathed until the voice of the Rabbi rang out in ancient blessing and the spell was broken.

Later, many friends and family joined the brides under the Chuppah and read words to express their feeling. From a Shakespearean sonnet to Marge Piercy's poem, "The Chuppah," to personal words written by the readers—all were like gentle strands weaving a mantle, covering us together with Barbara & Beth.

The Weaving

Linda Diamond

From a square on the Chuppah
at Barbara and Beth's Wedding

Betty Dorr and son Michael.
Photo: Bob Dorr

Witness

Betty Dorr

I was the final witness in the church trial of Jimmy Creech at Kearney, Nebraska. Reverend Creech is senior minister of First United Methodist Church of Omaha, Nebraska. I testified on Friday, March 13, 1998. I told the story of my family and my church. It turned out to be a lucky Friday the 13th.

My brother came out as a gay man to me and my husband Bob in 1959. I was very fortunate to have a mother who believed in unconditional love. Thanks to her, I was able to understand and accept my brother as a very important part of our family.

Then in 1966 my brother-in-law came out to us. The love and acceptance that we had been raised to believe in reminded us that our family members are children of God, as we all are.

We have three sons. We are a very close family. Over the years as our sons were growing up, they were active in our United Methodist Church. Two sons are married and we have two grandchildren.

In 1992 our youngest son, Michael, came out to us during a trip to Omaha to attend his best friend's wedding. He knew we would continue to love him because he knew that his two gay uncles were loved.

He said, "Mom and Dad, I know that you love me, but when I walk out the front door who else will? My church has told me that they feel it is wrong and so does society."

That was when I joined PFLAG. At first I asked myself, "What can one person do?" Now I know.

I attended national PFLAG conferences and received training to organize a Speakers Bureau. At first I spoke only before small groups.

I also became active in the Reconciling Congregation Program of the United Methodist Church. In 1996 I attended the General Conference of the United Methodist Church as part of a group called Open the Doors. We wanted the conference to know that there were people who advocated for inclusion of gays and lesbians in the church.

We didn't prevail. One statement was added to the Social Principles. It read: "Ceremonies that celebrate homosexual unions shall not be conducted by our ministers and shall not be conducted in our churches." Later in 1996, our church in Omaha included the words "sexual orientation" in our Vision Statement emphasizing that all were welcome. That statement was approved unanimously.

I was raised as a Baptist. My husband and I have been married for 41 years, and we have belonged to First United Methodist since we moved to Omaha 38 years ago. We have been proud of our church. It was on the leading edge of the race relations issue in the 1960s. We have been active church members. I taught Sunday school, worked with the youth choir, and served in the women's society and on many church commissions. My dream has been that some day my entire family would be fully accepted in our church.

In July 1996, a new pastor, Jimmy Creech, was assigned to our church. As Jimmy was preaching his third sermon, I realized to my amazement that I was hearing a sermon on love and acceptance of gays and lesbians. I felt that he was talking just to me as he told me he believed that lesbians and gays were being rejected by the church.

Jimmy came to a PFLAG meeting at my request. He said that it was important for people who were committed to each other to celebrate their love with a covenant service. Two women in our group asked him to perform the service for them. He did that on September 14, 1997.

My husband and I couldn't attend because we were in Orlando, Florida, for the National PFLAG Conference. When we returned home we learned that several people were upset. They planned to file charges against Jimmy. At the PFLAG conference, I attended a workshop on faith. I was able to testify in the trial knowing that many people were standing at my side.

In my testimony I said, "I love my church and the Methodist history. My dream is for my son to be able to celebrate a long-term relationship with someone—to have someone to love and care for.

"My son's gay sexuality is a gift from God. Our churches must take on the responsibility of studying, learning and accepting our gay, lesbian, bisexual and transgendered members. I dream of the day when our gay son will fall in love and come home to celebrate his covenant ceremony in our church.

"I would love to worship openly with my family and extended family of gay, lesbian, bisexual and transgendered people.

"My dream has started because, thanks to Pastor Creech, my brother is now attending church with us after 45 years of not going. I know gays that would love to come home to their churches if they felt accepted."

The church trial jury, made up of 13 United Methodist ministers in Nebraska, found Jimmy Creech innocent of violating provisions of the *Book of Discipline* when he conducted the covenant ceremony.

In the five years that I have belonged to PFLAG, I have added to my family sons, daughters, and parents from all over the United States. I speak not only for my son and his partner but for many others as well. There have been a lot of tough times, but when I hear, "Hang in there, Mom; we love you," from one of my "adopted" gay treasures, I know I am doing the right thing. They need to know that there are pastors and lay members of churches who care for them and that they can come home to their church.

Editor's note: Reverend Jimmy Creech was not reappointed as minister of First United Methodist Church of Omaha, Nebraska. He had a second trial in Nebraska in November 1999 and was found guilty. He and his family returned to Raleigh, North Carolina where he is accepting speaking and preaching engagements around the country. He is also writing a book about his experiences in Omaha.

Spreading Light

Irma Fischer

Three years ago I didn't know or care about homosexuals. When I got pensioned after 30 years of work in a pharmaceutical firm, I decided to completely change the course of my life. At that time I imagined a big open gate through which brilliant light could be seen, and I saw myself walking towards that light. It was a very strong, continuous vision. So I began to work with my church and an orphanage, thinking that these things represented the light that was calling me.

Then I learned of my son's sexual orientation. He was 27 years old, living in Germany. I always had a good relationship with my son, Robert, who lived in Argentina until his 24th birthday. He was a quiet, reserved boy, with a lot of girlfriends (just as friends), but very few boyfriends. Robert even had a steady girlfriend in Argentina, and I thought she would be my daughter-in-law one day. Then everything became different. Robert would never marry this girl. But I still saw him as an honest and lovable son—a wonderful person. And I realized how much he must have suffered during all these years, and that he needed my love and understanding. I also contacted a wonderful parents group in Germany, both by phone and in-person, and was helped tremendously by them.

I began to investigate what existed here in Buenos Aires, Argentina. Little by little I came to know gay groups and gay people. I saw that there was no real parent group here. And together with another mother, almost two years ago I founded the Parents Group in Buenos Aires.

It is hard work. Parents aren't showing themselves easily. But very often we receive calls, even of young gays, and the mere action of telling us about their problems and taking their burden off, makes them show an immense gratefulness.

I began to realize that the help we can give is infinite. How much despair, desolation and loneliness there exists! Every time I give my comfort, I feel that all our effort is not useless.

My son helped me with my first steps. Our bond to each other is stronger than before. There doesn't exist any more hiding from this unknown subject which restrained us from complete openness and understanding. I accept him as he is, and we can talk about everything. He is my dear, reliable friend.

Now I have the strong feeling that I wouldn't miss this experience in my life. It made me know a new world, experience my emotions, and feel needed like I never felt before. I even think that destiny played a part in my son being gay, so that I could start this new path in my life, so necessary for many people.

I realize that I am walking in the brilliant light I only saw as a vision before. Only now this light is connected with my son's life, with our relationship, and with the life of many people who need help. Every action of dedication, help, listening and comforting is immersed in this light.

My father always said about my mother, "When she enters into the room, the sun begins to shine!" I hope that I may be able to spread some of the light which I am now receiving!

For all this, I am grateful to my son!

Coming Out at Home

Ellen and Harold Kameya

With wondrous delight we greeted you
That rainy night in October.
Sixteen long hours of labor
Then . . . a beautiful gift from God.

Our daughter Valerie came out to us as a lesbian in 1988.

Valerie Mieka, we named you
Meaning: brave, beautiful, graceful child.
You grew into a magical person
Kind, sweet, smart, and gentle.

Eleven years later in 1999, *we* finally came out to our second-generation 83-year-old parents. It took 8 years in PFLAG, and we were able to do it from a position of strength and unconditional love! Our coming out to them was liberating for us.

A miracle! God's miracle.
Each birth brings tears of joy.
Each tiny one born in His image
Beautiful child. Precious child.

A few months ago, we visited my parents on the island of Maui. I had heard that my childhood church, the Iao Congregational Church, was possibly going through the process of declaring themselves to be Open and Affirming to Gays, Lesbians and Bisexuals. That surprised me since the small town of Wailuku with a predominantly-older Asian population was not noted for any social activism.

My beautiful, precious child,
What will I teach you of life?

To love God, truth and justice
To always be true to yourself.

We visited the church in May. It felt strange to see my 4th grade
teacher and my Sunday school teacher still active in church life.
As I met the minister in the receiving line, I asked him if his church
was investigating the Open and Affirming process. He said that
it was true, and I handed him a business card with the words "Parents, Families and Friends of Lesbians and Gays" on it. His eyes
opened wide and his smile became even wider. "Come, you must
meet some people!" he said excitedly, as he led me toward one of
the leaders of the project.

I thank you for being my teacher
You have done an incredible job
I have learned that being different
Is just another way of being.

The leaders were very excited to learn of our availability as
resources. For many of the local Asian population, homosexuality is not an Asian issue. The church leaders knew that having an
Asian face associated with the issue would make a greater impact.

A journey! Your journey.
Proudly I watch you fly.
May peace be your life companion.
May you know life's deepest joy.

We now feel that it would be unconscionable to *not* speak out
in support of gay, lesbian, bisexual and transgendered people.

A dream! Our dream
Of a kind and gentle world
Where every mother's precious child
Sings out in life's circle of love.

Christian Olson (right) and his partner, Tom Feddor.
(see also article by Nancy Lamkin Olson on pages 77–78)
Photo: David Edelfelt

Alleluia

Reverend Kurt Olson

"Mom, Dad, I have something to tell you."

"Okay, son, what is it?"

"I'm gay."

"We know."

"I thought you did."

"So, how come you're telling us now?"

"I've met this wonderful guy, we love each other and I want you two to meet him."

"Marvelous. Let's have dinner together, the four of us, this week."

This is how our son officially came out to us six years ago when he was twenty-three. Quick, simple, painless, a real celebration. I know that many parents of homosexual children do not respond in this manner. We did. And we want millions of parents to know that all is not *sturm und drang* being parents of a gay kid.

Our son and his partner have been together for six years. They've had their challenges like all couples do, and my wife and I continue to celebrate both of them every day. Our children, like all children, have been created in the Creator's image. Most world religions teach that and cite the first chapter of Genesis in the Bible as a proof text, especially Islam, Judaism, and Christianity.

I have been a priest in the Episcopal Church, USA, for almost twenty-five years. A few years ago, while worshiping at St. Thomas's Episcopal Church in New York City, I heard Hopkins' words put to song. These words speak to the depth of my soul.

"Oh, God, I love thee, I love thee—Not out of hope of heaven for me nor fearing not to love and be in the everlasting burning . . . Nor for heaven's sake; nor to be out of hell by loving thee; nor for any gains I see; but just the way that thou didst me I do love and I will love thee: Why must I love thee, Lord, for then? For being my king and God. Amen."

Why must I love my son, for then? Because he is made in the

image of my king and God. Amen. Coming out, being one's true self is an act of faith, not just in oneself, and in others, but in God.

Our very first experience with the Creator is in our own creation. The act of creation is always an act of love. Whenever I see any of our three kids, I feel so proud, so delighted that they're in this world. They honor life simply by being. Their presence is a joy. That my children are in this world is celebration enough for me to rejoice unto eternity.

No child can receive too much praise or too much love. No child, regardless of his or her age, is too young or too old to be shown—and not merely told—how very precious and wonderful he or she is. A huge part of my sense of worth shines forth in the gems I am privileged to call my children. My best task as a father is to reflect back to my kids their innate worth and integrity.

Good religion, true religion, does not condemn, but always upholds, always celebrates life and always invites God's creation to a closer relationship with God. We all "belong" in God's bosom.

For many people the journey towards celebration of their child begins with toleration and moves towards acceptance before coming to the ultimate: celebration. John Donne, the Anglican priest and seventeenth century dean of St. Paul's Cathedral Church in London, reminds us that each individual's joy is joy to me, and each person's dream is my own.

When I march in the Chicago Pride Parade and hear and feel the joy and love coming forth from all the gay, lesbian, bisexual, transgendered, and heterosexual people both in the parade and in the crowds watching, I get a big glimpse of what I think heaven is like: creatures cheering for the creation in all its fullness.

When the priest prepares the altar for Holy Communion, he mixes the chalice with a few drops of lustral water and says, "O God, who has created humankind in Your image, and has more wonderfully redeemed humanity . . ." This is meant to convey that when Christ again returned to the Father after His resurrection he took the whole of humanness into the Godhead for eternity.

My son's "gayness" is part of the Godhead. That alone is more than enough to celebrate with my whole being. Thanks be to God. Alleluia. Alleluia. Alleluia, Amen!

V

. . . AND ALL WE DID WAS LOVE

Joseph Basile (left) and his brother Steve.

Loving Every Minute

Joe "Papa Joe" Basile

On October 17, 1992, Steve appeared at our house for one of his surprise visits. My wife was cooking meatballs and there was a chill in the air.

For the first few hours Steve was like a hen on a hot griddle. We knew something was up, but we didn't quite know what. His mom thought he lost his job. I was concerned that he made some girl pregnant! My old school Italian upbringing was conjuring up thoughts of how quickly we could arrange a wedding! Little did I know how far from the truth my worries were.

When all the hectic activities (which are normal in our house) calmed down, Steve came into the kitchen, and said, "Mom, Dad, I have something to tell you. I'm gay."

The worried, almost fearful look on his face, made us both go to him. We hugged him so tight that we almost choked him.

He told us that he left his suitcase in the car because he thought we might put him out! The guilt and shame that I felt at that moment are hard to describe. Where did we go wrong? Didn't we let Steve know how much we loved him? Did we ever give him the impression that we loved his siblings more? Did we ever do anything to lead him to believe that we would ever stop loving him?

Steve told us he had just been to Washington where he visited the Names Project AIDS Memorial Quilt. It was there that he realized he could no longer live a lie. He could no longer continue to hide who he really was, and in fact who he really is.

Our family has always been very close, and since Steve came out to us on that October day, the bond between us has become even stronger. He has shown me that a man of 71 with his macho Italian upbringing, a man who normally has his opinions cast in steel, can become a tolerant, giving, understanding human being. He has helped change me from a man who told queer jokes (and was quite good at it) to a guy who will not allow anyone in his presence to hint at telling one. He has shown me that I can cry in the company of other people without feeling any shame. He has allowed me to hug and be hugged by perfect strangers, and love every minute of it. He has introduced me to a group of gay and lesbian people, who are loving and giving.

We thank Steve many times over for being honest with us and with himself. We also thank him for allowing us the freedom to love him for who he is—even though I may never forgive him for thinking that we would toss him out.

Maybe the reason this upsets me is because it exposes a glaring shortcoming on my part. One which makes me feel we did not tell Steve often enough how much we loved him. Believe me, we certainly make sure to tell him now.

We both have since come out to our friends and relatives. We have rainbow flags on both cars, and we jump down the throats of anyone telling gay jokes or trying to talk down about "those kind" of people.

If you bring children into this world, you *must* nurture them and you *must* support them. Most of all you *must always* love them.

Steve will always have our love, our devotion and our support.

Mother's Day

"Laura Lamb"

On the Saturday night before Mother's Day, my beautiful 17-year-old daughter arrived home from an evening out with friends. She curled up at my side and I lightly stroked her hair as she recounted the highlights of her evening. One thing led to another, and she looked at me and said, "Mom—I have something to tell you."

I asked, "What is that, dear?"

And she answered, "I like girls."

This one confession got under my radar completely. The telling of it was so unexpected that it caught me off guard and held me still for one second.

So I handed her the only olive branch I could. Love unconditionally. I kept right on stroking, and right on holding. I asked a thousand questions, and she answered them all. We ended the conversation with a kiss good-night and reassurances.

I spent Mother's Day tiptoeing around my house, taking sideways glances at my daughter. Something felt different but everything looked the same.

I became a parent when I first conceived of my daughter, underneath a full moon at a Sarah Vaughan concert in Rochester, New York. That wasn't when I got pregnant; it was when I first thought of her as mine. That hadn't changed.

Later she gave me a hand-made card. Inside there was a note that said:

"Love makes a Mother—not the ability to conceive." She went on to say that she was celebrating me—her mom.

How can I not love every inch of her?

Not a Boo in the Bunch

Reverend Bob Hawthorne

Pick a date—any recent year, just so it's June. Thousands of people are crowding Market Street, packed together for the San Francisco Gay, Lesbian, Bisexual, Transgender Pride Parade. We are part of the large contingent marching under the purple and white banner of PFLAG. It's intoxicating.

Every year I'm amazed. We're ordinary people who have done nothing more spectacular than loving our kids. Yet as we round the corner onto Market Street the cheers are deafening. The applause grows, on and on, block after block. There are shouts of "Thank you" and "Hi, dad." Smiles, tears, and above all, noise. Lots of approving noise, and not a boo in the bunch.

The contrast is what gets me. We have done nothing out of the ordinary, yet here's that unreal applause. And it goes on for the whole parade. I am saddened that it needs to be so, yet exhilarated that it is. We are the beneficiaries of something we did not earn. There is a peculiar grace, a touching generosity about that crowd.

Then the climax, for us. A parting in the crowd and our daughter runs out to join us, pushes her way through other marchers and links arms with ours. Our beautiful, lithe, vibrant daughter, with a smile that lights up the street. We three march the rest of the way pushing back the tears ourselves. It is a glorious moment.

Allison has given us far more than we could have given her. Our world has been expanded by hers. Her friends, gay and non-gay, have enriched us beyond measure. We have made new friends of our own because she is lesbian. Gathering with parents and gays, speaking on panels, celebrating at events have all made us more than we were.

Allison is a choice person. Her quick wit electrifies the family. Her love is near the surface, quick to overflow in an act or a tear. Her caring is a catalyst for the rest of the family. Her partner of many years brings wisdom and beauty to all of us.

So who should be cheering whom on Market Street? We are lucky—and all we did was love.

Telling Mom-Mom

Jean Lin

When your child comes out of the closet, one of the realities you are faced with is telling your parents that their grandchild is gay. You get to step in your child's shoes for a brief time. I found myself in this position after our son, Jeremy, told us that he was gay.

My mother has always been an open-minded person. She taught us by word and example that bias towards other people was ugly and unacceptable. Growing up in Florida in the fifties and sixties and traveling throughout the south, we often encountered blatant racial prejudice. I remember the time my family walked out of a restaurant, after we had already begun our meal, because the host did not allow African-Americans to be seated. I left feeling very proud of my parents. My mom let us know that you should always treat others with kindness and respect, especially if the circumstances of their life, their religion or the color of their skin made life more difficult for them. My grandmother, my mom's mother, was a feisty woman with strong convictions. A staunch church going Methodist and devout Christian, she refused to accept the concept that some of her fundamentalist friends touted— that only Christians went to heaven.

"If my Jewish friends aren't going, I don't want to be there either!" she adamantly declared.

That's the background I came from, hardly a nest of bias. In addition, my husband Peter, is Chinese. Mom had welcomed him and his family with open arms, delighted to learn more about the Asian culture.

My mother is immensely proud of both her grandchildren, and very supportive of their activities and interests. She and Jeremy have always had terrific rapport, sharing the same honesty and wry sense of humor. She has been one of his biggest fans, flying out to see his high school and college theater productions.

On the trip to see my mom in North Carolina, I rehearsed how

I was going to tell her. The morning after I arrived we sat down with steaming cups of tea.

"There's something I really need to talk to you about," I said.

She looked worried, sensing my concern.

"Jeremy is gay," I said.

My mother visibly relaxed and smiled. "Oh, is that all? I thought something was wrong!"

She let me know that she had already guessed Jeremy might be gay, since we hadn't mentioned girlfriends in quite a while. She assured me that she had always loved him and always would. She let me know she was proud of my involvement in the educational efforts of PFLAG. We talked about the possible genetic components determining gayness. I asked if she knew of any other gay family members. She thought for a while and then recalled her favorite great uncle James, a bachelor professor, who lived with her family at various times when she was growing up.

"You know," she said laughing, "I think my mom was trying to tell me once that he was gay, and it went over my head. I just got it now!"

I told her that my daughter Jenny says, "Whenever you talk to people about gay issues, everyone seems to have a gay uncle!"

We laughed a lot that visit. An openness was created by our conversation. Our own special bond was reaffirmed, as we shared the unconditional love we felt for family. My mom said she looked forward to being with us all again in California soon.

The next time she came to visit we planned a special afternoon with the whole family in San Francisco, where Jeremy was now living. When we went to pick him up at his apartment in the Castro, we were immediately engulfed in the excitement swirling in the streets. It just happened to be the Saturday of Gay Pride Weekend! Jeremy, playing local tour guide, said, "You know, Mom-Mom (the grandkids' special name for her), there's going to be all kinds of exciting and crazy things going on tonight—the Dyke Parade, wild dancing in the streets, even some nudity."

She winked at him mischievously. "Well, it's too bad your parents are taking me back early, and I won't get to ring in on any of the fun."

It was so good to see the two of them—not missing a beat in the special joking camaraderie which was a hallmark of their relationship.

I've been called the stuffy one in the family by both of them!

After gorging ourselves over lunch at a favorite Shanghai restaurant, we went on to see the current exhibits at the Palace of the Legion of Honor.

The grand finale of the day was reveling in the beauty of a sunset over San Francisco Bay. While waiting for the sun to go down, Jeremy pulled out a photo of Jamie, his very special British boyfriend. He showed it proudly to his grandmother.

"I can't wait to meet him. I've always loved that name and wanted a Jamie in the family," she smiled.

As I watched the two of them happily chatting over the photo, I felt an enormous gratitude for the enduring quality of a grandmother's love, and for a heritage which believes in affirming all our human differences with genuine appreciation and joy.

Peter Gambaccini (left) and Paul Gambaccini.
Photo: Darren Cheek

The Bond Between Brothers

Peter Gambaccini

In a recent network TV movie starring Glenn Close as an un-closeted lesbian, Col. Margarethe Cammermeyer, her artist love, played by Judy Davis, is, to her extreme dismay, "outed" on the national news. Immediately afterward, the Davis character, who had worked to keep her sister uninformed about her sexual proclivities, gets a phone call from this sibling. After hanging up the phone, she tells Cammermeyer that her sister always knew she was a lesbian: "She was just afraid to say anything because I never did."

As my brother Paul and I can both tell you, decades of sibling closeness can be squandered by such unresolved issues. An un-acknowledged fact had grown into a big rift between us. Only the truth could bridge the gap. Finally, when Paul and I were both on the far side of 35, I reached across the lunch table and, without preamble, broached the obvious but unspoken: "Are you gay?"

Paul looked startled, then relieved. "Partly," he said, but as our conversation continued, it became clear that "partly" was not the right answer. Finally, we'd breached the gap. No longer would we have to dance conversationally around what mattered. We could confide and be close. Brotherhood was rekindled.

Long before that lunch, I was virtually certain that Paul was gay. Which only left me to wonder why he didn't think I could handle knowing it. My credo is the last line of Mark Harris's "Bang the Drum Slowly": "From here on in, I rag nobody."

I'm a holdout against the notion that gender, race and sexual preference define us absolutely. Neither do they automatically toss us into two antithetical camps. My most competent editor is a black lesbian. What we don't have in common doesn't obscure what we do share. It's possible that on a list of 10 likes and dis-likes, a random straight person and a random gay one may con-cur on nine out of 10, differing only on the matter of whom they'd like to sleep with. I'd always had that 80 or 90 percent overlap

121

with Paul, which made the chill between us all the more un-
fathomable.

This was the brother with whom I'd played thousands of back-
yard Wiffle Ball games. We'd figured out who should buy which
British Invasion albums and divvied up our Batman, Aquaman and
Fantastic Four comics. We went to the same schools and church,
took the same family vacations and had the same boyhood sports
idol, Lakers' forward Elgin Baylor. There are catch phrases that
only we share. I knew this guy.

When Paul was 12 (and I was 11), we were inseparably chummy
with another pair of Italian-American brothers, the Tomassis.
They moved away when their father was transferred, which was
when Paul slipped out of my life, too. The door to his room was
hardly ever open to me. We never walked to junior high together.
After I watched him play baseball, he would wander off the field
alone, never noting my presence. Our only closeness came when
we took the same side in Sunday's heated dinner table arguments
—strongly for civil rights and adamantly against the Vietnam War.
Politically, we didn't disagree on anything. I don't think we do
today.

I hadn't made much of the fact that he rarely dated in high
school; I didn't date *at all*. The torment and trauma of a very strict
religious upbringing had left us ashamed and afraid of our feelings; I thought any girl I touched would denounce me as a pervert.
We pretty much got the same message that any potential mate
must be as pious and virtuous as Bernadette of Lourdes.

For two years during college, Paul and I lived on opposite sides
of the same university quadrangle. He never sought me out and
never made eye contact. He would literally backpedal whenever
he saw me. I assumed he disapproved of my being far more coun-
terculturally profligate and a far less diligent student than he was.
After college, Paul didn't desire much contact with the family
either. During brief visits, he would rush out of the house on assorted flimsy pretexts. When I first visited Paul in England, he ignored me as if I were invisible. A glutton for punishment, I kept
coming back for more.

What I'd observed about Paul meant I knew him like no one else
did. In films of his first Holy Communion, the other kids are fil-

ing in quite casually, but Paul's praying so hard he's nearly busting a gut.

In the 1980s, on his biennial visits from London, Paul would appear in New York accompanied by mute young men on whom he doted. At restaurants, he would whisper an undercurrent of commentary to them, ignoring me. It was getting annoying. Why count me out?

Finally, this fraternal relationship's returns diminished to the point of intolerability. Our failure to openly acknowledge his homosexuality created a wall between us that couldn't be scaled. To eradicate it, I had to yank him out into the open.

That was then. On a more recent Thanksgiving, my girlfriend and I spent the day with Paul and perhaps his first truly significant other. In the evening, we joined our younger brother, Phil and his wife and family for dinner. It was the first time all three couples had been together. Later, Paul and his partner shared their first "PDA" (public display of affection) in my presence, which touched me more than anything. He was sharing his life with me. (I was touched again, in sadder fashion, when he later told me of the sundering of that relationship.) To be moved by these things, all you have to be is human.

There still are family members with whom Paul hasn't discussed his sexual orientation, but I'm glad I'm not one of them. Our relationship now works because I forced the issue and because we're close in age and even because of our adopted hometowns. Paul and I live in the cities (London and New York) that are, in spite of their numerous flaws, two of the most polyglot and tolerant metropolises in the English-speaking world. We believe in that "gorgeous mosaic" stuff.

With each visit, details of our mutual backgrounds rise up to be examined, and hopefully at long last, understood. And while most of my old running mates race toward conservatism in middle age, Paul and I are both unreconstructed, unrepentant lefties. We're family, we're attached, and no matter of sexual orientation is going to end that.

We both cherish Christmas at Phil's home. We both dote on our enchanting niece, Katy. Backstage, Paul introduced Katy to the Broadway cast of *Beauty and the Beast*. We each do what we can.

A Parent Genie

Donald J. Moran

Imagine that you are a "Parent Genie." You can make one wish for your child that will come true in his or her lifetime. Not the traditional three or even two, just one majestic desire limited only by your imagination. And since you are the parent, you get to choose the golden wish.

Thoughts of fame, fortune and celebrity status race through your mind. Unlimited riches, fabulous beauty, political power are all at your command. Your child could be more wealthy than Donald Trump, more beautiful than Elizabeth Taylor. Why not President? At the very least, a successful neurosurgeon or the greatest athlete ever. The selections are boundless; anything you conceive is possible. But remember only one wish is permissible.

Although money and prestige are desirable, what other factors should I consider to make my child's life most complete and rewarding? Have I overlooked some of the more fundamental joys that are the essence of a full and fruitful life? Let's begin with personal happiness. Is that not more enriching than all of Trump's casinos?

How about pride? Isn't a deep personal pride more important than a Nobel Prize? To truly know and be proud of oneself is more profound than any of Einstein's theories!

Well fortunately my child possesses both pride and happiness, so I will have to consider other rewarding fantasies.

Let's not overlook health, both mental and physical. Once again, fortune has been more than kind. Genetics indicates a long and vibrant life.

Perhaps a successful business career. Again my wish would be squandered. My daughter developed her own incredibly prosperous enterprise without any family intervention. Even her graduate degrees were the result of her own energy, perseverance, and earnings.

Wouldn't you want your child to experience the quintessential goal of living—to truly love and be loved by a lifetime partner? Again, no need for "Parent Genie." My daughter cherishes and is showered with love and respect by her incredibly supportive wife.

You see my daughter is a lesbian who is brilliant, successful, married to a woman and undeniably happy. Her dad is the proudest father, her biggest fan, and loving supporter.

Michelle, also known as Quirk, is the nationally known founder and president of the world's largest gay and lesbian computer online service. Featured on America Online as onQ, Michelle's audience has been estimated at over eight hundred thousand people.

What more could any parent hope for than to know his daughter is delightfully happy, healthy, living a compelling life of love and commitment with her chosen partner, and contributing more to her fellow man than she receives?

Anyone care for an unused genie wish?

What a Waste

Karen Torgerson Jackson

I had a day with my wonderful, beautiful daughter, and we
didn't say much at all about being gay. What a waste. You'd
think I'd have given it more thought, spending so little time
together as we do, living so far apart and all. One whole day. We
could at least have concentrated on what's important.

What did we do? Nothing, really—our day that could have been
so meaningful. Hours over a pot of good coffee (bought special
for her visit), punctuated by FedEx delivering a chocolate heart
and the keys she needed to get back into her car. My daughter's
engaged, you know, fairly recently, and still toying with the ring,
peeking down and turning her hand to catch a sunbeam on a
diamond—then smiling. I totally forgot to ask her partner's view
politically, frittering the time instead on what she's like. We've
never met, but she plays guitar, loves to cook, adores *Toy Story*—
putters in the garden, skis like a champ, collects miniature Japa-
nese teapots. I never asked a thing about how she feels being a
lesbian. Just distracted, I guess, and pleased with how happy my
daughter looked piling detail on detail (you know how women can
go on).

I could have suggested something lesbian for the afternoon. I'd
planned the coffee; I could have orchestrated an itinerary. Instead,
a whole half hour in a candy store giggling over Gummi sharks
and tart raspberry jellies, sneaking chocolate-covered pretzel bits!
It's almost embarrassing, but we went shopping—and not even
gay-oriented establishments. Hours we idled in "regular" stores,
trying on slacks, sharing tastes in underwear. I introduced her to
my tailor, and she saw me beam when he complimented a "European taste." Not a word about gay or straight, the focus instead
on cuffs or no cuffs.

Rather than delve into identity, we got lost, as city girls can do
on the back roads of Indiana. The only orientation we discussed
was direction, and she was right: the turn she'd taken was west.

Then we talked about tiling her bathroom, sponge painting walls, who minds the dog while she works. I listened to what it feels like to tell a patient her unborn child won't be okay, and what terrible gas mileage you get with a sports utility vehicle.

My daughter wanted to cook for me (not that she totally avoids meat), so we went to the grocery store. I meant to ask if she truly felt celebrated, and not just accepted, but I'd never really looked at fresh beets before, and what is this thing called fennel? As she cooked, she said she bought a new kitchen faucet, just like mine. And her house might be a little small, maybe they'll get a big house in the mountains, definitely a second dog. Not a word about being gay, but a lot about good times to visit Northern California. And holding hands, the seconds ticking, saying nothing.

One whole day with my wonderful, beautiful daughter, and we never said much at all about being gay. Just together, just for a day, a daughter and a mom. Truly a waste, but oh, so special, just to be. Even the silence, especially the silence, resounding with love.

Designer Genes

to my daughter, Samantha

Sondra Audin Armer

My mother has no sense of style
and never did.
She bought clothes much too big
I could "grow into,"
but had no skill at sewing,
never hemmed the skirts
or took in drooping dresses.
Short and scrawny,
I disappeared inside the folds of fabric.
I'm still a runt, but chunkier,
and when I'm dressed to kill
an APB goes out to the fashion police.

I tried to pass this pattern on to you,
but somewhere in your DNA was lodged such flair
that even in your teens
you could pick up a thrift-shop sweatshirt,
rip out half the stitching,
and seem to wear the look from some exclusive boutique.
You knit, embroider, quilt,
create your clothes
so that you're always beautifully turned out,
and over all you've turned out so beautifully
that when it comes to love,
you've got mine all sewn up.

VI

I KNOW THAT YOU LOVE ME
BUT WHEN I WALK OUT THE DOOR
WHO ELSE WILL?

Sol and her two moms:
from left, Joann Kelley, Sol Kelley-Jones, Sunshine Jones.
Photo: John Quinlan

Testimony of a Really Lucky Kid

Sol Kelley-Jones

(Sol, at age 10, recited her written testimony before over 500 people at a legislative hearing on a statewide anti-same sex marriage bill in Wausau, Wisconsin on March 10, 1997).

Hi, my name is Sol Kelley-Jones. I am ten years old. I'm a really lucky kid because I have two parents who love each other and love me very much. My parents are always helping me and lots of other people, too. My friends tell me how lucky I am because I have always had a mom home with me after school who fixes great snacks. Not everyone is lucky enough to have two great parents so I know I have a lot to be thankful for. Some people don't understand everything about my family—like having two moms.

They ask me, "Who is your real mom?" I say, "They're both my real moms." I have a great family full of lots of love. That's why it's hard for me to understand why people are so afraid of us that they want bills like this. I don't see any way that this bill helps families, and it hurts my family a lot.

I read the signs carried by some people who support this bill. They say things like, "God hates gays and lesbians"—that our family is bad. This is scary for me. Once last year we went to a church service where people were carrying these signs and yelling at us outside. I woke up crying that night, because I dreamed that these same people bombed our church and our family was there. I don't want to be afraid of these people and others who support this bill and I don't want them to be afraid of me. I think we can all get along. We don't have to be exactly the same way.

In my history class in school, we've been studying about the beginning of the Constitution of the United States. As legislators, you know that it says that all people are created equal and have the right for the pursuit of happiness and equal protection under law. Well, I've been learning about Elizabeth Freeman, who was an

131

African-American slave owned by one of the drafters of the Constitution. As a slave she didn't have any rights. Elizabeth Freeman couldn't get legally married and her kids could get taken away from her. Today, my parents also can't get legally married, and it's scary for me to know that, if one of my parents died, I could be taken away from my other parent.

Two hundred years ago, Elizabeth Freeman went to the government and asked for her rights—like it said in the Constitution. Some people hated or feared African-Americans so much that they would have changed the Constitution rather than allow Elizabeth Freeman her rights. They said terrible things, like if African-American people were freed and had equality under law, everything Americans believed in would crumble. Elizabeth Freeman won her freedom, the right to legally marry and to protect her children. And America didn't crumble; it got better.

I know that there are people here today who will say the same kinds of things about my family that they were saying about Elizabeth Freeman and her family. From studying history, I've learned that our Constitution does not say that "all people are equal, except for gay and lesbian people and their children." It says "all people." As an elected official, it's your job to uphold the principles of the Constitution against hate and fear.

I'm sure it took a lot of courage for the legislators back then to give African-Americans the right to legally marry and to protect their children. For my sake, and the sake of hundreds of children like me, I trust you will have that kind of courage today.

Thank you.

A Grandfather's First Pride Parade

Margaret DaRos

This was our fifth Pride March—our fourth in Portland, Maine, the home of our PFLAG chapter. We also participated in the memorable March on Washington in April 1993.

Marching in support of equal rights for gays, lesbians, bisexuals and transgendered persons had become a familiar event for us as a family—my partner Dennis and our sons, John and Jeremy. Portland Pride on June 21, 1997, however, was different. That day, marching alongside us were my 73-year-old parents. Just 6 years ago we feared they might not be accepting of John as their gay grandson. It was not that my folks were uncaring, heartless persons. Quite the contrary. It was more the anticipation of rejection we contemplate when coming out to those we love. I especially remember having this concern when I first began to share with those closest to me that John was gay. We, however, are blessed with compassionate, loving friends who continue to celebrate John and our family without reservation. However, there is a fairly common belief associated with coming out to the grandparents—the belief that members of their generation will not understand and that it is best to "keep the secret." The grandparents are often last to know or they never know. For John, the decision was not whether to come out to his grandparents, but when and how.

I remember the difficult, early weeks after John told us he was gay on Thanksgiving Eve, 1991. Even my background as a psychotherapist and Dennis's as a diversity consultant did not prepare us for the jolt that can come from acknowledging our child was different. Many of us observe life through a heterosexual lens. We assume that our children, like us, will be straight. I worried that if this were a difficult process for us, how would our parents cope?

My fears were ill-founded. They, too, experienced a time of adjustment, but their love for him never wavered. My Dad shared stories with us, telling how he would speak up if he heard deroga-

133

tory remarks about gays. My Mom asked how she might obtain an address for the television program "Ellen" so that she could express her support. She also sent John and his partner a Valentine card to celebrate their relationship. They were more than accepting—they were embracing.

About a month prior to the Portland Pride March, I invited my parents to join us for the weekend's festivities. I was delighted that they accepted our invitation and surprised to learn they actually wanted to take part in the parade. Participating in a politically active event would be totally out of character for them. My parents are people who keep to themselves and value their anonymity.

On the morning of the march, we arrived early at Portland City Hall Plaza where the preliminary rally was to be held. The master of ceremonies requested PFLAG members in the audience join him on stage at the top of the granite steps to City Hall. The theme of this year's event was "Family Values," and we were asked to introduce our families to the crowd prior to the introduction of the guest speaker, Candace Gingrich. With some degree of anxiety and a great deal of pride, I addressed the 200-300 persons who had gathered, announcing we were "3 generations strong" marching in Gay Pride. I introduced each of my family members and John's grandparents, John and Eleanora Perry, who received tremendous applause. I stepped back as Mom and Dad waved to the throng, representing those grandparents who were unaware, unable or unwilling to attend.

As we began the progression down Portland's main street, the people lining the street were joyous and appreciative of PFLAG's presence. My parents had the opportunity to experience the love and appreciation of the gay and lesbian people who stood watching the parade pass. Then a curious thing happened. As we reached the end of the procession, a group of veterans stood outside a city hotel. This group of twenty or so, expressed their disapproval through stern stares, crossed arms and intermittent jeers and verbal assault. As we reached the end of the parade, my Dad shared the anger and hurt he felt after receiving such a reception from his veteran peer group.

The next day, my Dad who had returned to his home in Massachusetts called to say he had written a letter and wanted our opinion before he sent it on to our local newspaper. Dennis answered the phone and was first to hear its content. He was touched deeply by his words and both were teary as they shared the moment. The following is the text of the letter:

Dear Editor:
This is the first time I have ever written a letter to a newspaper. I hope you will see fit to publish it.

Yesterday, Saturday, June 21st, I was in Portland, your fair city, to attend a parade and festival put on by the gay and lesbian citizens of Maine. I had never been involved in anything of this sort, being a heterosexual male 73 years of age, married 50 years, this year. My grandson, however, is a 30-year-old admitted gay young man. He is fortunate in that he is supported strongly by his parents and his many friends and associates.

I felt that my wife and I should, to show our love and support, join my daughter, her husband and our gay grandson in their walk through the city to the park. I was amazed at the enthusiastic reception that the friendly people who lined the parade route accorded us. The warmth and goodwill they demonstrated was far beyond any expectations I might have had.

Then at one point near the end of our walk, as we approached what appeared to be a hotel, I became aware of a group of veterans, in full regalia, lined up in front of the building. I believe many of them were accompanied by their wives. As we, a small segment of the parade made up of parents and friends of gay children, passed the veterans, we were glared at with such hostility and hate as I have never before encountered in my life. I wondered, is this the look that my grandson encounters from some segments of society anytime he makes his sexual orientation known? How sad! Were these people, in their minds, standing tall for "family and the American way"? Was I, in supporting my grandson who is dear to me, representing evil?

To those veterans I say, my wife and I love our grandson. We and his parents could not have asked for a nicer boy. Our grandson did not ask to be homosexual; I did not ask to be heterosexual. The die was cast, the cards were dealt, and we must play the hand that was dealt to us.

I ask these people, what would you do in our situation? Would you cast the boy out of your life? Would you order him to change his sexual orientation? Or would you go to the pharmacy to see if you could get a special pill to "cure" him? I choose to love him and support him. To do less would not make me much of a man.

I would add, I am a veteran of World War II, having served for 35 straight months in combat areas of the South Pacific with "C" Company, 754th Tank Battalion.

Sincerely,
John Perry

The willingness to make a public statement in support of his cherished grandson is the kind of behavior we all must engage in as friends and family of the gay persons we love. As allies, we have a powerful voice. I applaud my Dad's speaking up and speaking out.

As I reflect on this and the many events, opportunities and moments we have shared since John first uttered the words, "I'm gay," I and we as a family have been blessed with a gift. We have experienced a deeper, emotional bond as a family. We have grown personally and professionally. We have even at times felt the pain and terror of oppression and discrimination. But most importantly, we know that we live the true meaning of loving and valuing family.

My Daughter—the Teenager

Becky Sarah

When my daughter Cory turned 15, she announced, "Mom, I'm lesbian."

My plan was to join PFLAG right away, and go to the Gay Pride march with them. I always liked PFLAG—devoted parents, supporting and helping our kids, working in a grassroots way against prejudice. But until I had a lesbian daughter, I had no connection to the group, no reason to be part of it.

I know some gay and lesbian children really appreciate their parents marching in the parade and I naively thought Cory would feel the same way. We had been having all the conflicts that 15-year-old girls and their mothers usually have, so it was nice to look forward to something we could agree on. Something that would work well, something I knew how to do right. We could march together!

But NO! Cory was horrified.

"You can't go," she screeched. "*I'm* going to Pride. People I *know* will be there. I don't want my *mother* to come."

It was worse than the time she was in 3rd grade and I was asked to bring our golden retriever puppy to visit her class.

It was worse than the time I offered to talk to her 5th grade health class about childbirth.

It was worse than my wearing sandals with socks in public all her life.

I think I was the only mother wearing her PFLAG button on Pride day but not going to the march out of deference to her lesbian daughter's feelings.

Now she's 18, living on the other side of the country, much more grown up, and she thinks it's funny, too.

"I was *so* adolescent back then," she says. "Next time we are in the same town on Pride March day, we will walk together."

This wonderful daughter has always been the light of my life, but she sure is easier to enjoy now that she's not a teenager any more.

Hineni*

Lauren Hauptman

Answer: Because the sun rises and sets on my little brother. Question: Why is a straight woman from New York running a San Francisco gay and lesbian newsmagazine? In fact, why the hell is the straight woman from New York even in San Francisco in the first place?

I told you: Because the sun rises and sets on my little brother.

The day Michael came out almost five years ago, my life was irrevocably changed. The world was no longer safe for my little brother, and it was my job to change that. No question. No hesitation. I had a brand new reason for living.

I read and I watched and I listened. And then I yelled and I screamed and I marched. I joined PFLAG, and I came out to cab drivers and people at the bus stop. I starred (okay, maybe I wasn't exactly the star, but I like to think I was, so humor me) in a PBS documentary called "Mom, Dad, I'm Gay" with the rest of my family—the self-proclaimed "Cleavers of the '90s." I volunteered with GLAAD (Gay Lesbian Alliance Against Defamation) and the Hetrick-Martin Youth Center, for gay, lesbian, bisexual, transgendered and questioning youth, and worked as senior editor of *POZ* magazine.

For the past four years, on the last Sunday in June, I have cried continually down Fifth Avenue through Greenwich Village in the delirium that is New York's Pride Parade. I cry for the kids who ask my parents if they can have a hug because their parents have disowned them. I cry because there is still only one day a year for Pride. And I cry because I am so proud of my family, of my brother, of every gay, lesbian, bisexual and transgendered person who has had the courage to come out and simply be who they are. And I cry for those who can't.

---

*pronounced: hee-nay-nee, Hebrew for "Here I am."

While I may not be able to walk in my brother's shoes, I will sure as hell march beside him, holding his hand, screaming at the top of my lungs (you may want to consider ear plugs). It is my responsibility—no, my mission—to change the world. Too lofty? Maybe. But that is what needs to be done and that is what I plan to do.

So here I am.

Because Michael met Bob and they moved to San Francisco and I was heartbroken.

So here I am, editor-in-chief of *San Francisco Frontiers Newsmagazine*.

Professionally, I will do my absolute best to produce an entertaining and informative magazine for the community. Personally, I will do anything necessary to protect my little brother. Without him, the sun would neither rise nor set, and it would be very, very dark.

I hope the sun shines brightly on the gay community—on Pride day and every day.

Something Joyous Within Me Broke Through

Betty Cornin

My daughter Nicole has been punching at boundaries since she was a child.

At the age of nine, she was the first girl to go to Summer Trails, an all-boys baseball camp. When she went with her younger brother for his tryout, she insisted that they permit her to try out as well. Surprised by her ability, they were reluctantly forced to accept her. The whole thing was her idea.

Nicole is an original thinker blessed with the courage to act on her convictions. I have always been proud of her.

Nicole is a lesbian. I have also learned to be very proud to have a lesbian daughter. Because of her, I have been inspired and challenged to do things that have enriched my life.

It was June 1989, the twentieth anniversary of Stonewall, and we were attending a PFLAG meeting. A fair amount of time at that meeting was spent planning for the upcoming Gay Pride celebration. When PFLAG invited us to march with them in the parade, I hastily declined. I explained that I'm not a joiner by nature, that I hate crowds, that I never even became a member of the PTA at my children's school.

A woman who had remained quiet during most of the meeting tentatively raised her hand and identified herself as Silvia. She was slender and attractive and was probably in her 70s. She spoke softly with a European accent. She reminded me of my grandmother. She said she wanted to tell me a story. I had to lean forward to hear her words.

"There are many groups that march in the parade. There are all the religious groups, then there are all the ethnic groups. Then there are all the crossover groups of transvestites, bisexuals, s/m guys and gals, the Black Catholics, the Irish Catholics. There are professional organizations. There are artists groups, writers groups, political groups, the disabled, gay veterans. A kaleidoscope of groups. But always groups. Nobody is without a group. About ten years ago, during the march, a small schoolteacher named Jeanne, held a sign she had made herself which said, 'I Love My Gay Son!' She marched alone. She was the only person who was marching alone. The following year, Jeanne returned, but this time when people saw her and her sign, a few suddenly stepped out of the crowd and fell in behind her, forming their own tiny group. That year there were five. When people saw this tiny group, the cheering was wild. The next year, there were twelve. The following year, there were seventeen. Each year more parents joined, some with banners, but all with pride. PFLAG was born."

Yes, the tears and mascara were running down my cheeks at the end of the story. I thought of the courage of this small, little woman to march alone, proclaiming her love and pride for her son. I was touched. I was impressed. But I still didn't want to march.

Two weeks went by and I awoke on the morning of the march knowing in my gut I was going to march with Nicole. Armed with a bottle of water on my shoulder, khaki Bermuda shorts, and baseball cap, we set forth. It was crowded and hot at the starting site of 63rd St. and Central Park West. It took almost two hours before everything was organized enough to begin. The atmosphere was jubilant and friendly. We found PFLAG and I was warmly welcomed by familiar faces from the meeting. But I was miserable and sorry I had come. "Okay," I reasoned to myself, "I'll march for twenty minutes, say I'm tired, and drop out." Nicole sensed my discomfort and kept asking if I was okay.

As we slowly began to move, the energy began to shift. We moved from 63rd Street onto Central Park West and slowly began to make our way towards Columbus Circle. As the momentum of the march increased, something joyous in me broke through and overtook my mood. I started to feel a sense of rightness and immense pride. The people packed onto the sidewalks screamed, waved, and blew kisses at us. Nicole and I, who were holding hands, waved back and raised our fists into the air. At one point, Nicole and I carried the PFLAG banner by ourselves. I was brimming with pride and love for my daughter. This was also her first time marching. To be sharing this moment with her was magical.

Midway through the march, my daughter turned to me and said, "I'm getting tired. What do you think? Should we stop?" I thought to myself, "Is she insane?" and said, "We are finishing this march together." She was surprised and said, "Okay! Don't get excited!" She had thought I was looking for a way out. When we passed by Macy's on 34th Street, a woman in her 50s, wearing beige pumps and carrying a Macy's shopping bag excitedly joined our group. "I had forgotten the march was today!" she exclaimed. "My daughter is gay and she lives in Pennsylvania. I just finished shopping but I have to march for my daughter!"

When we finally turned the corner onto Christopher Street, the cheering for our group was like thunder in my heart. People were on rooftops, hanging over fire escapes, leaning out of windows, and squeezed along the sidewalks. Kids were running apace with us crying, "I love you." "I wish you were my parents." "My parents threw me out." "My parents hate me." My entire body was tingling with the collective hum of joy and love in the crowd. Tears were streaming down Nicole's and my faces. Without question, it was one of the most powerful experiences of my life.

The process of coming to celebrate my daughter's lesbianism stretched me as a human being and helped me grow in courage and commitment. It takes a lot of strength for our children to come out. But if we really want to help them, we have to come out too.

I am an elementary school teacher in Queens. Everyday I play Scrabble during my lunch break with some of the other teachers who are my friends. One day, someone casually mentioned the Rainbow Curriculum. Annette responded, "What the hell is the Rainbow Curriculum?"

Marsha explained, "It's a program they want to put in the schools to teach the kids about fagillahs and dykes."

My friend Sally reacted, "With all that we have to worry about, now we have to worry about teaching them about gays!"

I answered, "What's wrong with teaching them about gays?"

Suddenly everybody was listening.

Then I asked the group, "Have any of you actually read the Rainbow Curriculum?"

"No, have you?"

I said, "As the mother of a lesbian, of course I've read it."

This was my official coming out.

I continued. "The Rainbow Curriculum teaches about all kinds of different families. And gay and lesbian families are just some of the families it includes."

There were many gasps and shocked looks and curious questions about which of my daughters was gay. We'd all eaten lunch together for twenty-three years and thought we knew everything there was to know about each other. Suddenly an issue that seemed to happen to other people was affecting one of us.

Softly and stammering, in a high nervous voice, Dolores said, "My eldest son is gay."

Another gasp went around the room.

"Oh my God, I don't believe it," several women responded.

Teachers are very isolated. The only time they have to form a community is at lunch time. It took a few days for people to become comfortable enough to ask, but then the questions came pouring out of their mouths. From time to time after this, somebody would broach the topic either asking a question about lesbian or gay life and behavior and now there were two of us in the room who were able to give information. They were very interested to know how the grandparents reacted, how the other siblings reacted. They wanted to know if the clothing of my daughter had changed, if she was dressing differently, if she had cut her hair. They wanted to know if I permitted my daughter to bring her girlfriends home. I responded by pointing out that if I let her bring her boyfriends home, why wouldn't I let her bring her girlfriends home? As the year progressed, I noticed a change in how these other teachers spoke about gays and lesbians. Their language and questions began to show a new understanding and respect.

In order to make the world a better place for our children, we have to dispel myth and ignorance, educate, illuminate, and eliminate homophobia. I do this by talking in my small sphere, making my voice heard, talking in the teachers' room. I talk to my friends about my daughter, and her friends. I am out.

P.S. Imagine how surprised Nicole and I were two years after the parade, when we walked into the Duplex bar in the West Village, and saw a huge photo on the wall capturing our moment— the two of us carrying the PFLAG banner together!

Matthew Shepard (Dec. 1, 1976–Oct. 12, 1998).
Photo: Gina Van Hoof, San Francisco 1998

My Son Matt

Dennis Shepard

It's amazing what can happen to a person in a short amount of time. Two years ago Judy and I were wondering how our sons were doing in school and worrying about their future in this new, high-tech world. My biggest fear was that they would lose hope and give up. That they would be overwhelmed by the high cost of everything, be discouraged by the low wages, and be turned off by the impersonal, uncaring manner in which corporations seem to treat their employees.

Because Matthew was the oldest and would be the first to meet this "reality," I worried more about him. He seemed a poor fit for this dog-eat-dog world because he was too sensitive to other people's feelings, was not competitive in the business sense, and was much too idealistic. Unfortunately, it wasn't in my future to see what his future would become. Xenophobia stopped Matt before he could get started.

Xenophobia is a fear of foreign or strange people. Matt didn't know the word, and it cost him his life. He accepted everyone until they gave him reason to think differently. Being raised in Wyoming definitely contributed to that attitude. His mother and I did as well.

Judy and I were aware of problems in other parts of the country with people not being accepted because of their religion or skin color, but that didn't happen in Wyoming. With such a small population, Wyoming was a safe place to raise a family. Everyone got along, and there were minimal problems with "being different." Or so we thought. Now that I look back, though, I can see that the fear was there. I just kept my head in the sand and ignored it. All I wanted to do was raise my family, pay my house mortgage, and grow old without any controversy while I spent time with the boys and their families.

As Matthew grew up, there seemed at times to be an uneasy truce between us. I loved him with all my heart, and he loved me—but there was an occasional edge between us. Maybe I sensed that he was different without really understanding it. I look back now and realize that I continually tested him to see how he would react. Was it due to disappointment that he wasn't six feet tall and a great athlete? Was it that he never seemed to be interested in the things I liked? I don't know. Was it that I was afraid he might be homosexual? Perhaps. I now wonder how many other fathers have done the same thing and have never accepted their son or daughter because he or she was different. (Xenophobia begins at home.)

Don't get me wrong. I was extremely proud of Matt's accomplishments. His quick wit and his abilities to meet people and make instant friends, to act in college- and adult-theater group plays, and to learn languages made me realize that I had quite a son. No matter where I was in the country, I never missed a play or an award ceremony. I also coached him in soccer and in the Cowboy State Summer Games, held every year in Wyoming, where he ran the five-kilometer race and swam the 50-meter freestyle. I did it because it was important for him and because of the memories and the bond that it built between us. I didn't know how much those memories would mean to me until later.

As Matt entered high school, I gradually came to accept the fact that he was and always would be different. I now know that this acceptance was what kept us close. Matt was my son, and I would never reject him. His difference made him what he was—a loving, sensitive, intelligent person.

As much as I looked forward to a long and loving relationship with Matthew, I also worried about him. Being overseas and so far away from him while he was in high school and college, I found myself wanting to call him daily just to talk and laugh. We still argued. (He was as stubborn and argumentative as his father.) In fact, we had a dandy of an argument on our last camping trip together. It didn't last long, though. They never did. By the time of that last camping trip, I knew he was gay. He had told me earlier that summer. He was rather surprised when I didn't react to the news. After all, Matt would still be Matt. It just meant that the possibility of grandkids had decreased dramatically.

Gay. Did you notice that a couple of paragraphs up I used the word homosexual instead of gay? I didn't know what the new definition of gay was until Matt was in high school. To me, gay meant happy, carefree, no worries. It wasn't that the term was new; it just had never applied to my family or friends. It hadn't affected my life, rights, or paycheck, so I ignored any reference to it. Typical attitude. I'd read something about gay rights or watched something about it on television, but it didn't mean much.

That all changed in October 1998. I never realized or appreciated how much Matt suffered physically, socially, and mentally until it was too late. To me, he was just Matt, just my son.

Smaller than most, Matt was athletic, but he participated only in individual sports. That way no one would have to depend on him to make the saving tackle or score the winning basket. He could run or swim at his own pace, stopping when he got tired or saw something interesting. He loved hunting and fishing for the same reason.

Because of his small size, he wasn't taken seriously by the "in groups" at school. He was in all the different social groups but was not a leader of any particular one. He knew everybody but had no close male friends, except for two boys who lived across the street. The three were inseparable until the last year or so of junior high, when differing interests caused them to drift apart. I think Matt knew then that he was gay but didn't know how to explain it to himself or to me. Definitely not to me! He didn't want to disappoint me.

At the time I didn't understand why he never had any male friends over. It's obvious now. His sexual feelings were different than those of the other young men around him. In his fear and confusion, he stayed away from them. His sensitivity and thoughtfulness attracted him to the distaff side, instead. He felt safe with women because they were easier in their judgment of his abilities and feelings. I, on the other hand, just thought he would come out of his shell soon and start dating.

Mentally, life must have seemed an incredibly impossible journey to him. How was he able to put up with the stresses of wanting to be himself and being too afraid to sit down and talk to me about his feelings? He continued on with his hidden life. Somewhere, I made a terrible mistake. Somehow, I closed my eyes to the fact that he was silently crying out to me to hold him and say that it didn't matter. Someday, I hope to have the chance to tell him how sorry I am that I left him to fight the battle alone. I only hope that other fathers open their eyes sooner than I did and take the stress and fear away from their kids. All they need is a hug and a kiss.

Like most people, I thought that it was all right to tell gay jokes —never realizing that every word I said helped build the xenophobia in the people around me. To me, the jokes were harmless. I told similar stories about myself, making me the butt of the jokes. They were like farmer or redneck jokes, not meant to hurt anyone.

It wasn't until I took a job overseas that I realized how bigoted I really was. No wonder Matt was hesitant about talking to me. I was totally shocked the first time I went to town in Saudi Arabia. Men walked down the street holding hands. And even worse, they kissed each other on the cheek—in public! What kind of society condoned this kind of behavior? What was I doing working with these perverted people? What kind of place was I trapped in?

What I was trapped in was my own moral code and closed mind. Saudi Arabia is a country with a culture that sees nothing wrong with male friends holding hands. They kiss each other on the cheek out of respect and friendship. Who was I to judge? That's when it began to dawn on me that people need to be respected for who they are. Tolerance was the greatest virtue, and I was intolerant as hell.

At the time of Matt's death, I knew nothing about the gay community and its issues. Matt never mentioned his campaigning in North Carolina against Jesse Helms. He never mentioned that he was living in a gay area of Denver. I met his friends and acquaintances, but never put two and two together. They were friends of Matt, so they were friends of mine.

Now, this isn't to say that I was entirely naive. As I stated earlier, I wondered at times if Matt might be gay, but I was afraid that if I asked him about it, he might say yes. I also was afraid he would be found out by people less tolerant than I was.

The first that I heard about gay rights issues and hate-crimes legislation was in the newspapers when I first arrived back in the States to go to Matt at the hospital in Fort Collins, Colo. Articles were saying that a national hate-crimes bill was needed to give legal protection to gay people.

Judy and I suddenly became spokespeople for something that we knew little about. We were immediately expected to know, understand, and discuss two issues that involved our son: gay rights, which Matthew worked for every day of his life, and hate-crimes legislation, which became so much of an issue because of his death.

Since Matt's death, I have read a lot about the arguments for and against hate-crimes legislation, and I believe it's something we need. When an entire section of the populace can be victimized with little or no recourse; when law enforcement agencies cannot draw on the resources of the federal government to investigate, enforce, and prevent crimes based on sexual orientation because those two little words are missing from the law; and when the majority of the country's population believe that sexual orientation should be added to the federal hate-crimes law but highly placed Republicans in the Senate and the House of Representatives refuse to listen to the voters and taxpayers, then it's time to get involved.

People, nevertheless, come up to me and say that this legislation isn't needed. They say it would give an unfair advantage to a special-interest group. They also tell me that there is no such thing as a hate crime—that all crimes are hate crimes.

When I hear this, I make the following suggestion: "If that's true, we don't need the hate-crimes laws now on the books to protect other people who have been singled out. Special laws protecting against discrimination based on religion, race or disability can also be eliminated. Get rid of them all. Let each incident be judged entirely on its merits." I usually don't get much of a reply to this suggestion.

I agree that a crime is a crime. I also agree that there are laws on the books to protect citizens against the normal crimes of murder, robbery, and so forth. However, when a group of law-abiding, respectful, taxpaying citizens is singled out and persecuted again and again, it's important for all people to say "Stop." Violence is being done to a group of people based only on their sexual orientation. This violence is physical, social, and mental. It's done publicly and privately. It's done without fear of repercussions. It's a form of discrimination that forces good, God-fearing people to stay home or move somewhere else to start up a new life. It's physical and mental terrorism, and it has to stop.

Hate-crimes legislation is not a cure-all, but it is a start. At the same time, the public needs to be educated. Gay people contribute so much to this country. They come from all walks of life and all backgrounds. They also seem to have an extra-special sensitivity, an awareness of the needs of other people and of their surroundings. I know this from being with Matt. What a bland, more callous world this would be if that sensitivity were to be driven out, repressed, or destroyed. We need to educate the country on contributions made in the past and on the contributions currently being made by gay people for the betterment of all Americans—not just gay Americans.

Since his death and the subsequent trials, I've had an opportunity to meet people—straight and gay—who adopted Matt as their own child or brother when he was fighting for his life in the hospital. Grief, shock, and horror know no boundaries. They cried with me then, and they feel my sorrow and loneliness today. I continue to be overwhelmed by the attention paid to me because I am Matthew's father. Many people thank me for the attention Matthew and Judy have brought to the nation and the world regarding gay rights issues. Others can't say anything and only cry. Some people come up simply to offer help and encouragement and to discuss the issues.

The hardest part for me is talking to the young people. When I see the kids, I see Matt—all enthusiasm and ideas and dreams. I also see something else that disturbs me greatly. These kids want to make their mark on the world, but it's clear that intolerance and bigotry have already started to affect their outlook.

A lot of them just want me to hold and hug them, and I'm thrilled to do it. It's like hugging Matt one more time. Many, but not all, are gay. I can't believe how many of them start to cry. Scared, most of them have no support at home and face constant discrimination at school or work. And when they tell me that Matt was lucky to have a dad like me, it makes me stop and think. I never realized before how many kids never had the kind of relationship with their father that Matt had with me. I feel so humble and so blessed.

These kids prove that the fight is not over. Judy and I are in this to the end. Judy will continue to focus her attention on education and legislation as well as on forums to keep gay rights issues in public view. I prefer to go after a more difficult target. I want to get fathers to realize that they are missing out on a huge part of their lives by not accepting their kids as their kids. I will continue to repeat one important message: "Matt was not my gay son. Matt was my son who happened to be gay." When other fathers can say the same thing, I will have accomplished what I have set out to do. Judy always tells the kids, "Be smart. Be safe." To that advice I would just like to add, "Be patient. Be proud of who you are."

CONTRIBUTORS

LIZ ARMSTRONG, a native of Los Angeles, has 3 children (her gay son died in 1993), and 4 grandchildren. She lives with her husband in Pacific Palisades, California and is actively involved in: PFLAG Los Angeles; GLIDE (Gays & Lesbians Initiating Dialogue for Equality), a speakers bureau; and Palisades Parents Together, a community network of parents supporting one another in order to create community and to become more effective parents.

SONDRA AUDIN ARMER's poems have been awarded prizes by Rita Dove and Margaret Atwood. Sixty have been published in literary journals, including *Sparrow* and *Western Humanities Review*, and in the anthology *Dog Music: Poetry About Dogs* (St. Martin's Press). She has taught English at five colleges and led poetry workshops at The Lighthouse (New York Association for the Blind) and other locations. Her daughter Samantha is also a poet and works as a doula, assisting mothers in labor and postpartum.

JOE "PAPA JOE" BASILE and his wife Jan live in Albany, N.Y. and have three daughters, two sons and six grandchildren ("five boys and one princess whom I spoil just a little"). When the topic turns to gay issues, Joe is "the first one to jump on the soapbox and start spouting off." One of his favorite quotes is "Many people talk the talk, PFLAG walks the walk."

EMILY BELL was 7 at the time of writing the letter to her grandma. She lives in Massachusetts with her mother where she is in the third grade at Bryant School. Emily enjoys sailing, flying, skiing, and the Spice Girls.

DEB BRIDGE teaches communications at Mount Royal College in Calgary, Alberta, Canada. She is married to Rick Dickson, an equally proud parent. Deb and Rick are deeply involved in the gay community and have become "Mom and Dad" to many. Their son, Michael Bridge-Dickson, is a National Ballet School graduate; in addition to dancing, Michael regularly performs as Ophelia Coxwell, and is best-known for his impersonations of Cher, Marilyn Monroe, and other divas.

PAT CAMPBELL is an educational researcher and the mother of Kathryn Campbell-Kibler. She was an expert witness in the Citadel sex discrimination case where her athletic ability turned out to be more important to the case than her expertise in statistics. That ability helped too when Pat and her husband Tom Kibler did the AIDS bike ride from Boston to New York.

VIRGINIA CHASE SUTTON has been twice nominated for the Pushcart Prize, and her poems have appeared in many literary publications. She has recently been a finalist for the National Poetry Series, the Walt Whitman Award, the Marianne Moore Poetry Prize, the New Issues Poetry Prize, and the Brittingham Prize. She has received grants from the Phoenix Arts Commission, the Arizona Humanities Council, and the Phoenix Public Libraries. Currently, she teaches writing at Phoenix College.

BETTY CORNIN is a teacher/writer residing in New York City. She is the proud mother of a straight son, a straight daughter, and a lesbian daughter. She has always believed that without societal restrictions we would all be bisexual.

MARGARET DaRos is a psychotherapist in private practice who lives in Harpswell, Maine. She is married and has two sons, Jeremy and John. She is a PFLAG member in Portland, Maine.

ANTAR DE SA lives in Palo Alto, California. He loves playing soccer and enjoys watching wrestling.

CELINA DE SA lives in Palo Alto, California. She likes reading, horses, dancing and soccer.

RASA DE SA lives in Palo Alto, California and looks forward to attending Storybook Camp next summer.

LINDA DIAMOND is an Occupational Therapist, active in the Gay and Lesbian Inreach Committee at her temple with her husband Norman. They have 10 grandchildren.

NORMAN DIAMOND, the father of two children, is a retired Certified Public Accountant. His involvement in the Human Rights movement through Temple Beth El of Great Neck, N.Y., expresses his good feelings to all gay men and women.

BETTY DORR was born and raised in Pueblo, Colorado and attended Colorado University. She worked as a classroom aide in the Public School System in Omaha, Nebraska. She is active in the Omaha Chapter of PFLAG.

IRMA FISCHER was born in the Philippine Islands from German parents. She has lived in Argentina since her parents emigrated there when she was 4 years old. She studied pharmacy and biochemistry, worked in a pharmaceutical firm for 30 years, married, had two children, a boy and a girl, who are both living in Germany now. She has two grandsons.

CAROLE (McLAUGHLIN) and RICHARD FOWLER JR. lived in Westfield, Massachusetts, where they operated the largest carrot farm in New England. They raised three sons and presently have their first granddaughter —the first girl in the Fowler family in 150 years. They live on the island of Nevis in the Caribbean where they continue to nurture orchids.

PETER GAMBACCINI has written for over 7 periodicals and is a regular contributor to *Runner's World*, *New York Runner*, and *The Village*

Voice. He is the author of five books including *The New York City Marathon: Twenty-Five Years.*

JENNIFER HARRIS is a graduate of the University of Toronto, living and working in Fort McMurray, AB. A diligent student of life in all its variety, this is her first piece for publication.

LAUREN HAUPTMAN and her husband, Jeff Weinberger moved to San Francisco from Manhattan, as she couldn't stand being so far away from her brother. Lauren is active in a variety of gay-related causes, and has served on the board of directors of PFLAG New York City and Under One Roof in San Francisco.

ROBERT J. HAWTHORNE has divinity degrees from Yale University and San Francisco Theological Seminary. He has served six Methodist churches in northern California and retired from active ministry in 1990. Bob and his wife of 51 years, Gene Anna, live in San Jose, California. Their lesbian daughter, Alison, is a travel agent in San Francisco.

SOL KELLEY-JONES is a young activist who does kid to kid workshops and teacher in-services in the schools to help people overcome homophobia and appreciate differences. She enjoys a happy home life with her two moms and dog, Sunna. Sol delights in the natural world, plays basketball, drums, and creates plays. She serves on the National Board of Children of Lesbians and Gays Everywhere (COLAGE) and spoke at the Millenium March on Washington.

HAROLD and ELLEN KAMEYA are members of Los Angeles PFLAG. Harold is an electronics engineer and Ellen is a school teacher. Both of them were born in the Hawaiian Islands.

MARGY KLEINERMAN lives in Brea, California. She is a retired elementary school teacher and has three children; her younger son is gay. She is active in the Orange County chapter of PFLAG. Her husband has Alzheimer's and is in a nursing home.

LAURA LAMB (pseudonym) was born in a small coal mining town in southwestern Pennsylvania. She was educated as a teacher and is currently working with special needs children. Her daughter plans on continuing her education after high school.

ABBY LAWTON lives in San Francisco, California with her two moms.

JEAN LIN lives in Saratoga, California with her husband Peter. She teaches Reading and English as Second Language classes for local colleges. She has two grown children, Jeremy and Jenny.

DVORA LUZ was born in Prague (1930). Together with her parents and brother, she succeeded in reaching Israel in 1939 where she has lived since. "When my younger son was 22, he came out to me. I was devastated . . ." But subsequently she became chairperson of PFLAG-Israel. The book, *Mom, I've Got Something to Tell You* (done by her and Sara Avni together) was published in Hebrew in Israel.

JEANNE MANFORD was raised in Queens, N.Y. She now lives in Daly City, California with her daughter and son-in-law. She has one granddaughter and two great-granddaughters. Jean taught elementary school and became active in gay politics in the early 1970s when her son Morty came out.

DONALD MORAN is the father of two beautiful daughters. One is a successful professional who happens to be lesbian; the other an accomplished housewife who happens to be heterosexual. He lives in Wallingford, Pennsylvania. A graduate of the Wharton School, he recently sold his businesses and spends his winters in Naples, Florida.

RHEA MURRAY founded a PFLAG chapter in Seymour, Indiana where she lives. She and her husband Butch are the parents of two children and two granddaughters. Rhea is a full-time college student, majoring in psychology and serves on the founding board for Community AIDS Outreach. She has published her autobiography, *Journey to Moriah*. Her passions, besides dancing and music, are exploring many different spiritual paths, writing, camping, traveling and boating.

MICHAEL NEUBECKER and his wife Janice (see front cover car photo) are the co-founders of the Downriver, Michigan Chapter of PFLAG. As proud parents of a gay son, who they credit with nudging them in the right direction, they now are gay rights activists without apology. They are the recipients of The Triangle Foundation "Pride Partnership Award" in 2000 and the "Spirit of Detroit" award in 1999. Their son Lee lives in Chicago and is the president of BuzzBolt.com, an internet service business. He is very proud of his parents' activism.

KURT ALLAN OLSON is an Episcopal priest and a psychiatric social worker. He is the former president of the PFLAG-Lakeview chapter. He is a tireless advocate for human rights and is the proud father of three sons, one of whom is blessed with the gift of being gay.

SHERRY PANGBORN is the parent of four, step-parent of two and wife of a Reserve Chaplain (United Methodist) in the U.S. Navy. She is active in two PFLAG chapters on the rural Kitsap Peninsula in Washington state. She says, "I am grateful to be the parent of a terrific lesbian daughter, who has opened our minds and hearts to a whole new world of wonderful people."

JAMES PINES has a gay son, a straight daughter and two grandchildren. He is a retired lawyer. He served as a U.S. Peace Corps staff member, and was an international development consultant. He graduated from

Bard College, Harvard (MA—economics) and Yale Law School. He is a member of PFLAG.

MELISSA PINOL has a BA in Social Science. She spent several years as an Employment Counselor for the disabled and has recorded books for the blind. She has also completed Rape Crisis Counselor training. She writes poems, stories and articles primarily for the Speculative Fiction and Metaphysical market, and has also written on woman's and disability issues. In addition to writing, she sings traditional music from the British Isles with a very talented Hammered Dulcimer player.

SHIRLEY POWERS is the author of *With No Slow Dance* (Two Steps In Press, Palo Alto, CA, 1980). Her work has appeared in *Matrix*, *Earth's Daughters*, *Iris*, *Iowa Woman*, and *Different Daughters: a book by mothers of lesbians*.

KIM ROBERTS is the author of a book of poetry, *The Wishbone Galaxy* (Washington Writer's Publishing House, 1994). Poems of hers have appeared in journals in the U.S., Canada, Brazil, France and Ireland, such as the *Ohio Review*, *Encontro*, *Sonora Review*, *Grain*, *New Letters*, and the *Plum Review*. She has received grants from the D.C. Commission on Arts and the National Endowment for the Humanities, and has been a writer-in-residence at artist colonies in Virginia, New York, Illinois, New Mexico and Wyoming.

DEAN ROSEN, Psy.D. is a clinical psychologist in independent practice in St. Louis, Missouri. He and his wife Louise are the parents of three children and are members of St. Louis PFLAG, joining their son in gay rights activities.

JYL SAFIER learned her activism and commitment to social justice from watching her mother organize a Metropolitan Community Church in Hayward, California, AIDS hospice groups, the San Francisco Gay and Lesbian Freedom Day Parade, and the San Francisco Women's Building. Jyl is a world traveler and particularly enjoys long-distance bike-touring. She also co-founded a local currency called BREAD (Berkeley Region Exchange and Development) and recently graduated from U.C. Berkeley.

BECKY SARAH is the mother of two grown daughters, and currently works in public health. Before studying public health she was a lay midwife and a natural childbirth teacher, and later an acupuncturist. She worked for several years in an infertility program that was the first in her area open to serving single women and lesbian couples.

GENE SHALIT is a self-described "movie critic" or "arts editor" or "You know, that guy with the bushy hair and mustache" on NBC's "Today Show."

DENNIS SHEPARD is a construction safety engineer based in Dhahran,

Contributors / 157

Saudi Arabia. He and his wife, Judy, became gay rights advocates after the October 1998 murder of their son Matthew. The couple, who focus their activism through the Casper, Wyoming-based Matthew Shepard Foundation, have one other son, Logan.

TOM STARNES is the retired pastor of the Chevy Chase United Methodist Church in Maryland. He is also a free-lance writer.

BONNIE SUBLETT lives in San Jose, California with her husband Roger. She is a retired school teacher and now serves on various government commissions. She is an avid horsewoman and competes in carriage driving events, most recently the Morgan Horse World Championship in Oklahoma City. Besides her three children, her Morgan horse, Mistress, is her pride and joy. She is also a gardener, reader, and avid people person.

KIA THOMAS was a 17-year-old student at Springfield Gardens H.S. in New York City when she wrote this article.

KAREN TORGERSON JACKSON lives in Chicago, writes for fun and for profit, and is actively involved in PFLAG. Her daughter, Anne-Marie Jackson lives in Santa Cruz, California, where she practices medicine, romps on the beach with her golden lab Bailey, and tackles more home-improvement projects than her mother can believe.

ELIZABETH VICKERY is active in a woman's club, poets society, aerobics and line dancing. She is widowed and has two daughters, five grandchildren and five great-grandchildren.

ALISON WEARING is a Canadian writer and calls herself "the proud daughter of a homo."

SONDRA ZEIDENSTEIN's poems have been published in *Taos Review*, *Women's Review of Books*, *Yellow Silk*, and *Earth's Daughters* and in a chapbook collection entitled *Late Afternoon Woman*. Fourteen poems are forthcoming in an anthology called *Passionate Lives* (Queen of Swords Press). She is publisher of Chicory Blue Press, a small literary press that focuses on writing by women past sixty.

DUNCAN ZENOBIA SAFFIR studied English and East Asian Studies at Lewis and Clark College. Now, he is a landlord-writer-sculptor who lives with his girlfriend's dog. For many years his entire family has been extremely active in Portland, Oregon PFLAG. Duncan is the 1998 NLA-Portland (National Leather Association—Portland chapter) title holder. Even as a heterosexual, he understands what it is like to be in a minority group and is very glad to have understanding and loving parents. Recently, he has had poems accepted for publication in various publications, and has had a chapbook, *All Romance Aside* (Future Tense Publications).

Laura Siegel.
Photo: Alan Siegel

Nancy Lamkin Olson.
Photo: Kurt Allan Olson

EDITORS

NANCY LAMKIN OLSON was born in Chicago, Illinois and was educated at Stephens College in Columbia, Missouri where she earned a B.F.A. in Theatre Arts. She is currently a retired professional actress who still pays her Actor's Equity dues religiously in the misguided hope that some day she will be "discovered."

Nancy and her husband, Kurt, a psychiatric social worker in a Chicago hospital and an Episcopal priest, have three sons. Her gay son has been in a committed relationship with his life partner for over 9 years.

LAURA SIEGEL received her undergraduate degree in biology and education from The City College of the City University of New York. She has published stories, articles and poems in magazines and newspapers including *The Sun*, *The Mindfulness Bell*, *On Parade '93: The Year of the Queer*, *The San Francisco Examiner* and *The Bay Area Reporter*. She has written and spoken about the joys of having a gay son since her younger son came out at age 19.

She currently serves on the board of San Francisco PFLAG (Parents, Families and Friends of Lesbians and Gays) and edits their monthly newsletter.

Laura and her husband Howard have two sons. Their younger son, who inspired this book, is a yoga instructor. Their older son, a first grade teacher, and his wife, recently made her a proud grandma, thereby giving new meaning to the word, dote.

RESOURCES

Parents, Families and Friends of Lesbians and Gays (PFLAG)
1726 M Street, N.W., Suite 400
Washington, D.C. 20036
E-mail: info@pflag.org
http://www.pflag.org

PFLAG Transgender Network (T-NET)
E-mail: KittenGR@aol.com

Children of Lesbians and Gays Everywhere (COLAGE)
San Francisco, CA 94110
E-mail: colage@colage.org
http://www.colage.org